Marriage:

The Way It's Made To Be

By

Ken Ortize

Marriage:

The Way It's Made To Be

By

Ken Ortize

Marriage:
The Way It's Made To Be

By Ken Ortize

© 1998 by Ken Ortize

Matters of the Heart Publishing
PO Box 28448
Spokane, Washington 99228

ISBN 0-9644634-1-5 (Second Edition)

PRINTED IN THE UNITED STATES OF AMERICA BY
GILLILAND PRINTING INC.
215 NORTH SUMMIT
ARKANSAS CITY, KANSAS 67005

All Scripture quotations are from the New International Version unless otherwise noted.

Table Of Contents

Acknowledgments

Whatever else might be said about an "acknowledgement", it is a clear admission that the book could not have come to its final state without the humble, and often selfless efforts of those who would otherwise remain unrecognized. Although the author is the primary creative agent, all books are essentially a collaborative effort.

I would like first of all to thank Dave Johnson, who produces my daily radio program, for first planting the idea of a book into my mind. He was among the first to believe the effort would be worthwhile.

Secondly, it was Don and Kim Stewart who showed how it could be done. Don, who has authored over twenty books, gave me both moral and practical insights on how to translate my words onto the written page. Kim, who provided design and layout expertise, was also a regular encouragement. Her "prodding" often got me restarted after temporary slow downs.

At just the right time, God provided Barb Flynn to edit and re-edit the text with loving corrections, carefulness to detail, and proper grammar and syntax.

The tedious and arduous job of typesetting was performed by Don Wiley. He patiently labored through numerous revisions and "changes of mind".

Lastly, and most importantly, I want to thank Jamie, my wife, my love and my partner in life. It was primarily the crucible of our relationship wherein this book was born. It was she who often assured me that I had something worth saying when I had serious doubts. She's endured my moods and my mania as I labored to birth this book; she's given up many, many evenings and weekends, as I hammered away on my laptop, oblivious to many of the needs she was left to attend to.

To all of the above, I recognize that "thank you" does not suffice. I know that you were motivated by your love of Christ and a desire to see this teaching reach others, that Christ might be glorified in their homes and marriages. Thank you for the honor of laboring with you in this effort.

...so in Christ we who are many form one body, and each member belongs to all the others... Therefore each of you must put off falsehood and speak truthfully to his neighbor, for we are all members of one body. Romans 12:5; Ephesians 4:25

A special thanks to Klundt & Hosmer Design for their help with this second edition.

1

Why Another Book
On Marriage?

Someone once observed that what motivates most students to study psychology is a desire for free therapy. I'm not sure that is always the case, but I know that's what motivated me to begin studying about marriage—my marriage was a mess.

My wife and I certainly never intended it to be that way. I doubt that anyone does. We were so self-assured, so confident, in the beginning. And why not? We felt we knew enough about being happily married to be successful. We had seen the latest release of "Romeo and Juliet," and our feelings seemed to mirror those of the lovers on the big screen. We were in love. And most importantly, we were both Christians. This proved to be our biggest misconception of all.

I remember my wife recounting to me a conversation she and her father almost had the night before our wedding. He sat her down and began to talk to her about some of the challenges she might encounter as a wife. Before he could even get into his comments, she quickly cut him off: "Don't worry Dad. We're Christians. We won't have those kinds of problems."

This proved to be a critical miscalculation. Being Christians did not even begin to address the lack of understanding we had of what it takes to make a marriage work. We barely knew what the Bible had to say about marriage, and what little we did know was not balanced by wisdom or experience. We were basically clueless about what marriage was all about.

Not surprisingly, our marriage soon became miserable for both of us, and for good reason. The adoring woman I had married had suddenly become a moody, critical and depressed nag. The strong and sensitive man my wife had married was now a self-centered, inconsiderate juvenile. We both felt tricked, deceived, defrauded and depressed. What were we going to do? To whom could we turn?

Like most other young couples, our thoughts eventually drifted toward divorce. We knew enough about the Bible to know that wasn't what God wanted. Neither of us had been unfaithful, yet. How would we explain divorce to our friends and families, many with whom we had been sharing our faith and were not yet Christians?

We slowly resigned ourselves to our fate. We concluded that our marriage was a terrible mistake, but for God's sake we would stick it out, "UNTIL DEATH DO US PART!" It seemed the only escape from this unhappy marriage was either death or the rapture. Neither of us wanted to do heavy prison time, so we began to pray, "Come quickly, Lord Jesus!"

As pathetic as this may sound, this was a vitally important step in the right direction. It gave our marriage the time it needed to begin the process of healing and rebuilding.

Now, 25 years and four children later, we laugh a lot more about it. Stories from our past have proven useful in helping others to identify problem spots in their own marriages. But, like an old wound, long healed, the scars of those days still remain—a constant reminder of the pain that once ruled our lives.

What follows in this book are insights which we have gleaned through the years by the help of the Holy Spirit, ministering through God's wondrous Word, through His people, and through one another. Every error and failing I touch on in this book is personally well known to us. What I share are our failures, our weaknesses and our sins.

Good decisions

Once a fledgling young executive asked the aged and experienced president of a highly successful business what the "key" was to his success. The older man responded, "Good decisions." Not being completely satisfied, the younger man countered, "But how do you make good decisions?" Without hesitation the older man shot back, "By making bad decisions."

If you gain any insights from this book, know that they have come through numerous mistakes, errors and bad decisions on our part. Over time, they have become insights—not insights which we discovered; rather they were revealed to us by a merciful God who answered us in our hours of pain and despair as we desperately sought for answers through His Word and prayer.

For the most part, we found the answers, not in the multitude of books on marriage (I have read too many) but in the Book of Books—the Bible. There are no quick fixes, simple steps, or clever formulas. I am convinced that making a marriage work is a life-long process, engaged in by two very sinful human beings. In the end, if it succeeds at all, it will be because the two aforementioned sinners surrendered their wills and pleasure to the Almighty God of the Bible, submitting to the life-long process of redemption, in particular the redemption of their marriage—a marriage created after the purpose of His will and for His good pleasure.

Happy or holy?

A few years ago, one of my lay leaders approached me with a question. He and his wife were in the process of forming an adult Sunday School class for married couples. They had spent months studying, researching and preparing for this class. On this particular day, he had come into my office with a brochure advertising a training seminar for laypersons involved in counseling married couples. The seminar was being taught by a well known Christian marriage counselor. The question my friend asked was simple and straightforward: "Do you think it would be a worthwhile investment for us to attend this seminar?"

As I reflected upon this question for a few moments, I quickly saw a critical point of distinction between what this seminar was seeking to accomplish and what we were pursuing in our church. I explained it to him this way: "I am sure this seminar is excellent. I am very familiar with the gentleman who is leading it, and I have read many of his books and benefited from them. But his objective is not the same as ours. He desires to help people build happy marriages. We desire to build holy marriages through holy lives."

The seminar was full of communication techniques and counseling models, all designed to help a married couple understand one another and get along more amicably. But it lacked a vital ingredient: the Word of God.

The Bible is not against communication. Rather, it approaches the issue from a different perspective. According to the Bible, the reason we have so much difficulty communicating with one another is because we have never learned to "speak the truth in love" (Ephesians 4:15). Instead we speak from "the abundance of our hearts" (Matthew 12:34), which is usually sinful and selfish.

When I think about communication techniques, I am reminded of a quip I once heard. It goes like this: "Sincerity is the principal thing. Once you learn to fake that, you've got it made."

I am not suggesting that we all are consciously deceptive or manipulative. Rather, it is something we do subconsciously. It happens naturally, inherently, out of a sinful, selfish human nature. It comes from a tendency to view our beloved as an object through which our needs and desires can be gratified. With such a perspective of the other, we easily see communication techniques and skills as a means of enhancing our own happiness, not meeting the needs of others.

What we need is not a new skill or technique but a new heart. That requires getting past our fear of true godliness as revealed in the way Jesus dealt with others. We must stop fearing to allow God to delve deeply into our hearts and change us from within. It means learning to pray like the Psalmist when he cried out in his desperation, "Search me, O God, and know my heart; test me and know my anxious thoughts. See if there is any offensive way in me, and lead me in the way everlasting" (Psalm 139:23,24). Essentially, it means desiring to be "holy" more than being "happy."

I have a right to be happy don't I?

Some of you may be having difficulty understanding or appreciating the distinction I have just made between holiness and happiness. I assume this because almost every married couple I have ever counseled has told me that their goal in counseling was to be "happily married." I have had many individuals in a moment of frustration declare, "I have a right to be happy, don't I?" They have always been surprised when I have very firmly and directly responded, "No."

You can study the Bible from cover to cover and you will not find a single passage that tells us that we have a right to be happy. Instead, you will find that the purpose of our very existence upon this earth is to glorify God, and often that is accomplished through times of pain, suffering and unhappiness. In fact, Peter cautions us not to view hardship as something strange or unusual: "Dear friends, do not be surprised at the painful trial you are suffering, as though something strange were happening to you" (1 Peter 4:12). And Paul correctly points out that married people will have troubles: "But those who marry will face many troubles in this life" (1 Corinthians 7:28).

I am convinced that marriage is one of the tools God uses to purify His saints. Purification takes place through the fires of tribulation. Peter describes the purification process as follows:

> In this you greatly rejoice, though now for a little while you may have had to suffer grief in all kinds of trials. These have come so that your faith—of greater worth than gold, which perishes even though refined by fire—may be proved genuine and may result in praise, glory and honor when Jesus Christ is revealed (1 Peter 1:6,7).

Even today, when metal smiths seek to purify ore, they heat it in a cauldron until the impurities rise to the surface. Only then can the impurities be separated from the molten metal and scraped away. Likewise, sufferings and hardships are God's way of bringing the "hidden things of darkness" (1 Corinthians 4:5) to the surface, that they might be recognized, repented of, forgiven, and by His grace, removed from our lives.

It has been my personal experience that marriage has been the most effective means in my life to reveal what a sinner I am and how gracious God is. It is marriage that has taught me the most about what it means to love unconditionally, faithfully and consistently.

Blessings are preferable to happiness

The Bible does not pave the way to mere personal happiness, rather it teaches how to be blessed. You may be wondering, "What is the difference between being blessed and being happy?"

Unfortunately, some Bible translations have not treated these two words with careful distinction. This has led us to believe that they are synonymous. Even in English they are not. For example, in my Encyclopedic Unabridged Dictionary, it defines "happy" as "favored by fortune; fortunate, lucky." In contrast "blessed" is explained as "divinely or supremely favored" which brings with it inner peace, contentment and feelings of happiness.[1]

If you look carefully, the difference is the source from which feelings of peace, contentment and pleasure are derived. "Happiness" depends upon outward circumstances, which makes it extremely fickle and difficult to maintain. "Blessedness" draws its happiness from God, despite outward circumstances. It is what produces the inner peace of which Paul spoke to Christians at Philippi when he wrote: "And the peace of God, which transcends all understanding, will guard your hearts and your minds in Christ Jesus" (Philippians 4:7).

Actually, the equivalent Greek word for "happy" (*euteches*) never occurs in the New Testament. Whenever we find the word "happy" in the New Testament, it is the translation of *markarios*. Greek scholar Spiros Zodhiates helps us understanding the distinction in terms this way:

> To be happy is to be favored by circumstances. A Christian and a non Christian may be happy, but only the born-again Christian may be blessed [*markarios*].
>
> The Lord Jesus never promised happiness based upon circumstances, but He did promise blessedness [*markariotes*].
>
> The word markarios also means "to be fully satisfied." When Jesus Christ saves us, God's nature indwells us (2 Peter 1:4) and because of that we are inherently satisfied no matter what the external conditions of life are.

To be happy is to have favorable circumstances, but to be blessed is to find full satisfaction in the indwelling Christ, and one is unaffected by the outward circumstances. It is to have the peace of God within in spite of possible affliction from without. The blessed person is one who is made satisfied because of God's presence within him no matter how much health or prosperity he or she possesses.

A happy person is one who experiences good luck. The word "happiness" comes from hap: chance; luck; lot—an occurrence or happening—even as the Greek word euteches which does not occur in the New Testament.[2]

When we apply this information to our marriages, we can begin to see how our own short-term desires have contributed to much of the unhappiness we experience in life in general, and in our marriages in particular. If our peace, joy, contentment, etc., is dependent solely upon outward circumstances unfolding the way we think they must, we will be frequently, if not constantly, unhappy. Life is too fickle and unpredictable for it to be otherwise, and marriage is a part of life, subject to the same influences.

Through the years, we all change, sometimes "for better," and sometimes "for worse." There is "sickness and health," "prosperity and adversity." Over time, we discover things about one another and ourselves that disappoint. Even the coming of children into our lives has a dramatic effect upon how we "feel" about our marriages.

Seasons of a marriage

Few unmarried or newlywed couples realize that the way they feel about one another prior to marriage bears no resemblance to how they will feel twenty years from now. They assume that the rather intangible emotions we call "love" will sustain them through all of the varying seasons of marriage.

Jane Aldous, in her book Family Careers—Developmental Changes in Families, has identified seven stages that predictably occur over the lifetime of a marriage. Each stage alters the level of satisfaction we feel in our marriages. She explains:

> The emotional euphoria with which most marriages start is eroded over time by establishing daily routines, by growing irritations from constant association, by competing attractions of jobs and children, and by coping with the multitudinous problems, both large and small, that family life in an industrialized society entails. Fortunate couples develop an intimate understanding unique to the relationship that replaces the raptures of the first period of the marital career.[3]

Today there are many competing ideas on what leads to a fulfilled marital relationship. Most of these stand in contradiction to the Bible; many are called biblical, but they are not. They may be sprinkled with Bible passages, but their foundation is modern, contemporary and secular.

What I have set out to do in this book is to present a true biblical basis upon which marriage can be built, as originally intended by God. I have used all the major passages of the Bible dealing with marriage as the framework around which this book is built.

I believe this is critical. We must become people who derive our understanding of all of life from the Bible, as God's holy, inerrant, inspired Word—the ultimate goal being that our marriages would do far more than provide personal happiness, that they would most importantly bring glory to God. It is in the pursuit of God's glory that our own is found (John 12:32; Romans 8:17). When pleasing Him is our desire, then we will know the pure pleasure of His will.

> You are worthy, our Lord and God, to receive glory and honor and power, for you created all things, and by your will they were created and have their being (Revelation 4:11).

2

Facing The Issue
Of Divorce

Some Pharisees came to Him to test Him. They asked, "Is it lawful for a man to divorce his wife for any and every reason?" "Haven't you read," He replied, "that at the beginning the Creator 'made them male and female,' and said, 'For this reason a man will leave his father and mother and be united to his wife, and the two will become one flesh'? So they are no longer two, but one. Therefore, what God has joined together, let man not separate." "Why then," they asked, "did Moses command that a man give his wife a certificate of divorce and send her away?" Jesus replied, "Moses permitted you to divorce your wives because your hearts were hard. But it was not this way from the beginning. I tell you that anyone who divorces his wife, except for marital unfaithfulness, and marries another woman commits adultery" (Matthew 19:3-9).

I t happens over a million times each year. It directly affects the lives of several million children and young people each year. The latest research indicates that it has a devastating emotional and psychological impact upon all who are touched by it. It is cited as the number one reason for the decay of the inner cities, rise of gang violence, and a number of other social ills. Yet we increasingly act as if it is just a normal part of life. Even within the church, we seem to have forgotten that God once said, "I hate divorce."

One of the most disturbing developments within the church over the last three decades has been the rapid increase of divorce among Christians. We have become accustomed to hearing about the ever-escalating rate of divorce in society as a whole. But the rate of divorce within the church is the same as that of non-Christians. According to the Barna Research Group, "In all, 23% of all Christian adults have been divorced. These figures are almost identical to those for the non-Christian population."[4]

Just a few decades ago, divorce within the church was almost unheard of. Not so today. Every pastor I know could give a list of members who have been divorced. One of the fastest growing areas of ministry is singles. The church's resources are stretched by the need for seminars on marriage, divorce recovery and parenting, especially single parenting. Pastors and counselors are overwhelmed by the number of couples and individuals seeking marriage-related counseling and support. An entire industry of Christian therapists and counselors has grown up to meet the ever-increasing demand for help. The best selling books in Christian book stores deal with the issues of marriage. Ironically, it seems the more we address the problem, the worse it gets. Have we become like those Paul described in 2 Timothy 3:7, "always learning but never able to acknowledge the truth"?

Divorce has even become more common among the clergy. The number of divorces among clergymen has quadrupled since 1960. In one ministry, 37 percent of the ministers they work with are considering divorce; and based upon precedent, 15 percent will dissolve their relationships.

If, as Jesus stated, "all men will know that you are my disciples if you love one another," what is the message we are sending to the world through our broken and loveless marriages? How does divorce enable us to be "salt and light" in our world?

One of the leaders in my church expressed the dilemma in a simple little verse. It reads like this:

> **If the difference that Jesus makes,**
> **Doesn't make a difference,**
> **What difference does it make?**

I am realistic enough to recognize that for those of you who are struggling painfully over your marriage one of the last things you are concerned about is how the non-Christian world views your marriage. For that I am very sorry, because I believe that is one of the reasons so many Christian marriages are failing. We have become so absorbed in our own feelings and issues that we are no longer concerned about living lives that are pleasing to God.

Just the same, that is why I have included the following section. In it, I seek to give you the facts about divorce so you can evaluate its true impact upon you, your children and our nation.

The true impact of divorce

You may be wondering, "Why start a book on marriage talking about divorce?" I believe that until we completely eliminate divorce as a possible option, we will not be able to fully commit ourselves to staying married. And if we don't commit ourselves to staying married, we probably won't. So let's continue by looking at some of the effects of divorce upon those whom we love.

Divorce is not just a matter between a man and woman. It savagely assaults their children, parents, grandparents, brothers, sisters, and friends. No one ever walks away from marriage and picks up where he/she left off. Divorce requires an entire restructuring and rebuilding of our lives. It is difficult to imagine that a person who fully understands the consequence of divorce would ever follow through with it. And yet, unfortunately, there is not a single one of us who has not been touched by the trauma of divorce and not come to know its painful effects.

Consider the following testimonial given by a member of my congregation on Sunday morning, as we were dealing with the topic of divorce. His name is Dan.

> Today in this room I would imagine there are very few people who can say their lives haven't been changed in some way by divorce. Whether it's been their own divorce, their parents, their brother or sister, a close friend, divorce is everywhere, and we can't help but be devastated in one way or another by this event.

In my own life, I have seen it happen to my older sister, my best friend, people I work with; but the divorce that hurt me the most was that of my parents. You see, my parents always seemed to have the ideal marriage. They loved and supported each other in their careers; they never fought in front of us kids and were always affectionate to each other.

But one night when I was 18, as I lay in bed reading, all that changed, and I wondered if I really knew my parents at all. My father, who had been in Greenland for a year with the Air Force, had just come home, and we were all looking forward to having things return to normal. But that night, I could just barely hear my parents having a discussion in their room. I wasn't even paying attention until I heard the word "divorce," and it made my heart stop. Surely they were talking about someone else! But as I listened closely, I realized that they were actually talking about it as a possible option for them. I couldn't believe it! They had always said their marriage was forever, that they would never even consider divorce. I'm not sure that when the word "divorce" was mentioned that night they were really serious about it. But once it was spoken, things went downhill fast. They began to fight openly, loudly, and often. The two people I loved most in the world, the people whose love for each other had been the anchor in my life, began to hate each other. It tore us apart to hear them say hurtful things to each other and know they couldn't stand to be in the same room together.

I began to wish that they would get a divorce so the fighting would stop. Yet, two years later, when they did divorce, I was devastated. I felt as though my parents had died, my family had died. I was twenty years old, and yet there was a little boy in me crying out, "This isn't fair, this isn't fair!"

I can remember thinking, "Now wait a minute. You said you would love each other forever and now you're quitting. Weren't you the ones who told me never quit? When the going gets tough, the tough get going . . . yeah, right out the door! You've just invalidated a whole set of values and morals that you'd given me! And if you invalidated those, I'm not so sure everything else you've taught me isn't also a bunch of garbage."

Now you may say, "Come on, you're being a little melodramatic about all this." But you have to realize, I had looked at these two people as my role models for twenty years. They were my set of standards I was planning to use, and now those standards were blown to pieces. I literally had to go back to areas of my life. I quit school, began drinking heavily and did a lot of very self-destructive things. And it took me a lot of years before I would take any advice from my parents on anything.

Shortly after their divorce, my older sister, who was married and had two boys, separated and finally divorced her husband. For years, my youngest sister wavered back and forth in her loyalty toward my parents. She thought she had to choose sides. My middle sister recently married and never even told my father. My younger brother was hit the hardest. His young adult years were filled with one tragedy after another. Instead of being supported and encouraged by the strength of my parents' love for each other, he saw two people awkwardly call a truce just so they could be there at the same time for him.

Because my father lives in Texas and my mother lives in Germany, we can't afford to visit them both. So we visit neither. My kids know who my parents are, but don't know them. My five-year-old doesn't understand why Grandpa is married to a lady who is not my mom.

The list of lives that have been affected by their divorce goes on and on.

That's why in the Bible it says, "What God has joined together, let no man separate." He's trying to keep us from all the pain and heartache of unnaturally separating something He has supernaturally joined together. Now, for those of you who may bear the scars of divorce, take heart. Even though God may allow us to suffer the consequences of our actions, He is a God of healing.

I wish I could say that Dan's experience was unique. But it is not. If you have been the child of divorce, you probably feel like Dan is sharing your story.

Count the costs?

How many couples really count the cost of divorce beforehand? For many years, well intentioned but ill-informed counselors advised struggling couples that it was better for the children if they separated. They "speculated" that children would be traumatized by viewing marital conflict.

What is tragic is that all this advice was not based upon fact. It was the "opinion," the speculation and false assumptions of these "experts."

Just the facts!

What are the true effects of divorce? One survey of 164,000 older adolescents provides us with a list of the hurts young people felt from their parents' divorce:

> Conflicts in loyalty to parents; feelings of abandonment and insecurity; depression; anxiety; difficulty concentrating on studies; sleep disturbances; increased dependency on roommates and friends; financial difficulties; difficulties with intimate relationships; eating disturbances; problems with sexual identity; withdrawal from friends and roommates; increased drug and alcohol usage.[5]

What was most surprising was the discovery that the older the person was at the time of his/her parents' divorce, the more devastating the emotional impact.

Another study by the Family Research Council[6] identified the following list of hidden costs of divorce:

• The poverty rate for children living in single-parent homes is five times the rate for children living with two parents.

• Divorced men experience an average 42 percent rise in their standard of living in the first year after divorce, while divorced women (and their children) experience a 73 percent decline.

• School-age children living with a parent and stepparent, or divorced mother only, are 40 percent to 75 percent more likely to repeat a grade and 70 percent more likely to be expelled from school.

• Children who grow up in fractured families are less likely to graduate from high school than children from intact families.

• A disproportionate number of runaway teens come from stepparent households.

• Young sons often experience nightmares and a "father hunger" soon after the dad leaves home. In their teens, they are more likely to have increased levels of aggression, gang membership and other emotional and behavioral problems.

• Young daughters of divorce often experience anxiety and guilt. In their teens, they are more likely to be sexually involved, marry younger, be pregnant more often before marriage, and become divorced or separated from their eventual husbands.
• Children of divorce typically experience depression, drug and alcohol experimentation and a diminished ability to form lasting relationships.

A nation in trouble

If all of this weren't enough, we need to consider the effect of divorce upon our nation. You can't throw a pebble into the middle of a pond without getting a "ripple effect." This is especially true with divorce, for divorce tears away at the very foundations of civilized society. When marriages fail, our entire way of life comes under jeopardy.

Only recently have we begun to hear much about the importance of family, as we have attempted to come to grips with the problems of gangs and the inner city. As these problems have reached epidemic proportions, social scientists and commentators have begun to notice the contributing effect of broken homes upon the social development of young men and women.

It was the 18th century historian and author Edward Gibbons, in his exhaustive history entitled The History of the Decline and Fall of the Roman Empire, who first identified several key factors behind the collapse of that mighty empire. One of the primary factors was the breakup of the family. Among the Romans, divorce had become commonplace. With the loss of stable families, the nation no longer was able to provide the kinds of leaders that were necessary to maintain the empire's position in the world.

In 1947, sociologist and historian Carle Zimmerman wrote a book entitled Family and Civilization.[7] He compared the disintegration of various cultures with the parallel decline of the family. He identified eight specific patterns of domestic behavior which typified the downward spiral of each culture he studied:

• Marriage loses its sacredness . . . is frequently broken by divorce.
• Traditional meaning of the marriage ceremony is lost.
• Feminist movements abound.
• Increased public disrespect of parents and authority in general.
• Acceleration of juvenile delinquency, promiscuity, and rebellion.
• Refusal of people with traditional marriages to accept family responsibilities.
• Growing desire for and acceptance of adultery.
• Increasing interest in and spread of sexual perversions and sex-related crimes.

Zimmerman concluded that when these behaviors begin to permeate a society, their effect is always lethal.

How does this compare with American society today? Columnist Margaret Hopkins in a recent article summarized it well:

> We are rapidly becoming a hedonistic society, embracing sexual permissiveness and perversion, filthy language, instant gratification, and looking to the government as the source "from whom all blessings flow."
>
> Violent crime rules our streets; pornography floods our land; teenage pregnancies swell the welfare rolls. Convicted murderers, child molesters and rapists are released to prey again on society. Drugs and divorce take their toll as families disintegrate. AIDS and sexually transmitted disease threaten the lives of our young people.

As one reads this appraisal, it has a clear ring of reality to it. It is as if a group of diabolical social planners used Zimmerman's list of social woes as a formula for societal restructuring. The future he warned about is here today.

The bedrock of civilized society

Why is the health of the family so critical to a society's well being? It is the foundation upon which everything else is built. A quick look back to Genesis reveals that the human community began with a man and a woman becoming "ONE." Jesus summarized it this way: "Haven't you read . . . that at the beginning the Creator 'made them male and female,' and said,

'For this reason a man will leave his father and mother and be united to his wife, and the two will become one flesh'? So they are no longer two, but one. Therefore what God has joined together, let man not separate."

The family is the place where we learn all the basics that will lead us through life. It is there we learn the skills which enable us to live with one another, to serve, to share, to care, to work together, to sacrifice for the common good. It instills within us the basic building blocks for civilization. Is it any wonder, when the family is fractured and children are left without healthy role models or parents who love and support one another, that we end up with a generation of young people who no longer know how to function in a civilized world as responsible and contributing adults?

Sometimes I shudder to think of what the future will hold for this great nation of ours. Yet, I am reminded that there are things you and I can do to make a difference. God has not left us alone. In fact, He has given us a mission. We may not be able to change or save someone else's marriage. But we can ensure that ours is the kind of marriage that not only blesses our lives, but also brings glory to God and stability to our nation.

But where sin increased, grace increased all the more (Romans 5:20).

3

Incompatible
By Design

And the LORD God commanded the man, "You are free to eat from any tree in the garden; but you must not eat from the tree of the knowledge of good and evil, for when you eat of it you will surely die." The LORD God said, "It is not good for the man to be alone. I will make a helper suitable for him.". . . But for Adam no suitable helper was found. So the LORD God caused the man to fall into a deep sleep; and while he was sleeping, he took one of the man's ribs and closed up the place with flesh.

Then the LORD God made a woman from the rib He had taken out of the man, and He brought her to the man. The man said, "This is now bone of my bones and flesh of my flesh; she shall be called 'woman,' for she was taken out of man." For this reason a man will leave his father and mother and be united to his wife, and they will become one flesh. The man and his wife were both naked, and they felt no shame (Genesis 2:15-18, 20-25).

I am convinced that Christian marriages have a far better chance of survival than those of people who exclude Christ from their lives, but if we are ever to experience the fullness of God's purpose for marriage, we must begin by committing ourselves to do whatever it takes to make our marriages work. This is not easy, for great marriages don't just happen. They are made. They are not the consequence of marrying the right person. They are the result of working hard to become the right person!

Through the years, I have observed two things about marriage:

1. I have never known anyone who at some time in his/her life did not desire to get married. That doesn't mean they succeeded. Many among us will live their entire lives as singles; some by choice and others by necessity. But we all have an inner drive toward marriage.

2. I have never known anyone who got married with the intention of getting divorced at some later date. There is a very simple explanation why this is so: God created us with the desire to be married. It's part of our basic programming. The only exceptions are those whom God has given a special calling to go through life as singles, as Jesus explained in Matthew 19:12.

Does that mean we are confident we will succeed in marriage? Apparently not, according to The Barna Research Group. In one study, they found that "While most Americans believe that God intended marriage to be for a lifetime, they also believe he doesn't understand the hardship that a difficult relationship causes. . . . A significant percentage of adults enter their marriage assuming that it will end in divorce; often, that is a self-fulfilling prophecy."[8]

The most troubling thing about this attitude is that it discounts God from the marriage process. We view God as a positive helper but not the one to whom we turn and rely upon for our basic understanding of what marriage and family life is all about. It is a lot like saying we love spaghetti but we hate noodles. If you take God out of the marriage equation, what's left? In most cases, two very lonely and self-centered individuals, who are desperately trying to convince, coerce and/or manipulate the other into loving them unconditionally. In most cases it doesn't work very well.

In the beginning

Many are surprised when I begin my marriage seminars by teaching from the first book of the Bible, Genesis, but Genesis is the book of "beginnings." It's like going to the manufacturer to find out how something was put together. If we are to understand how marriage is supposed to work, we need to go back to the one who originated it: God.

In Genesis, chapters 1-3, we learn three vitally important concepts:

- Chapter 1 tells us who God is.
- Chapter 2 shows us the primary purpose behind marriage.
- Chapter 3 reveals why being happily married is so difficult.

Who God is

In Genesis 1, we learn two things about the nature of God: First, that He is God and we are not. And second, that He is good. The book begins, "In the beginning God created the heavens and the earth." 1. This tells us that the God of the Bible is the Creator, the Sustainer and Maintainer of everything; He is the God who created "everything out of nothing," including you and me. 2. Secondly, we can also conclude that He is "the Almighty," the all-knowing, all-powerful, ever-present and everlasting God, and there is none beside Him. 3. And lastly, we see that He is the Sovereign God: superior and dominant over everything and everyone. He is the first and the ultimate authority.

What meaning does this have for us? As Paul tells the Ephesians, "In love He predestined us to be adopted as His sons through Jesus Christ, in accordance with His pleasure and will." We are the result of His creative energies and expression. We were created after the desire and design of His heart. We exist because of Him and primarily for His purposes and pleasure.

Until we understand and accept this truth, until we recognize that a truly purposeful and fulfilling life can only be found in God's will, we will spend most of our lifetimes struggling and striking out in innumerable directions, becoming increasingly frustrated and unhappy. Like one of my favorite adages says, "If you don't know where you are going, you're going to end up somewhere else." Until we realize that God created us to find Him and to live our lives in Him, we will never feel complete.

This is what Saint Augustine was saying when he wrote, "Thou hast made us for Thyself, O God, and our hearts are restless until they find their rest in Thee"; or Saint Francis when he wrote, "What a man is before God, that he is; nothing more, nothing less!" The Apostle Paul, when He spoke before the skeptics on Mar's Hill in Athens, declared, "For in Him we live and move and have our being" (Acts 17:28). It was the French physicist and philosopher, Pascal, who wrote that there is a God-shaped vacuum in the heart of each person that cannot be filled by any created thing but only by God the Creator made known through Jesus Christ. These great men discovered the central truth about life: Man's ultimate meaning and purpose is found in God; not in success—even marital success.

A successful marriage is meant to be an expression of our relationship with God, not a replacement for it. There is a tendency on the part of some today to so elevate the status of marriage that it begins to sound like the ultimate experience in life. Jesus warned, "What good will it be for a man if he gains the whole world, yet forfeits his soul? Or what can a man give in exchange for his soul?" (Matthew 16:26). Never forget that the primary and ultimate purpose in life is to have a relationship with God through Christ. The health of all our other relationships depends upon the health of our relationship with God.

Why is this critical for a happy marriage? Many times in counseling, I have discovered that couples are expecting their spouse to meet needs in their lives that only God can satisfy. Marriage cannot make me feel good about myself, or my life. I do not derive my identity from my marriage; marriage can never be more than the place where I express my identity. We become "idolatrous" in our attitudes toward our spouses when we begin to believe, even demand, that they be responsible for our personal happiness.

A basic principle I often share with single adults who are frustrated over their singleness is this: Until you learn to be content as a single, you are not ready to be married. Most of us, unfortunately, marry based upon our "needs." We assume our spouses will be the key to meeting those "needs." Ironically, many times we have not even identified what those needs are, but we sure enough know when they aren't being met!

Successful marriages occur when you have two people who are primarily givers, not takers. This is the essence of "love," as expressed by the Apostle Paul in 1 Corinthians 13:4-8:

Love is patient, love is kind. It does not envy, it does not boast, it is not proud. It is not rude, it is not self-seeking, it is not easily angered, it keeps no record of wrongs. Love does not delight in evil but rejoices with the truth. It always protects, always trusts, always hopes, always perseveres. Love never fails. But where there are prophecies, they will cease; where there are tongues, they will be stilled; where there is knowledge, it will pass away.

Some years ago, I had a young, single man come to my office to talk. He wanted me to review a list he had composed outlining the qualifications of the woman he would marry. To my utter amazement, his list was three pages long! Single-spaced! My response to him was two-fold: 1. The woman he was looking for didn't exist! 2. His attitude was one of arrogance and selfishness. He was only looking to how a woman could serve him, not how he could serve her. I told him, "When you are committed to 'being' the person you have described in this list, rather than marrying such a person, then you are ready for marriage, and not before!"

What God is like!

The most basic summary of God's nature is simply expressed by 1 John 4:8: "Whoever does not love does not know God, because God is love." It is for this reason we can know that God by His very nature is good and benevolent. He cares for the welfare of all He has created, especially mankind.

Genesis 1:31 continues the Genesis narrative by stating, "God saw all that He had made, and it was very good." Everything He created was designed to maximize mankind's personal happiness and fulfillment. His pleasure is to make us the recipients of His goodness. He desires to bless us.

Only when we accept the fact of God's goodness toward us will we be able to follow Him, to trust and obey His will for our lives. As King David expressed in Psalm 27, "I am still confident of this: I will see the goodness of the LORD in the land of the living. Wait for the LORD; be strong and take heart and wait for the LORD" (Psalm 27:13,14). David's ability to endure hardship was founded in His confidence in the goodness and perfect purposes of God for his life despite outward circumstances. We will never be able to experience the rewards and joys God has in store for all his children, the reward that comes to those who trust and obey Him, until we learn to have confidence in His goodness!

The primary purpose behind marriage

Genesis 2 expands the creation account by expanding on the creation of mankind. As we read through this chapter, there is one specially notable comment that should catch our eye. In verse 18, we read, "It is not good for the man to be alone. I will make a helper suitable for him." These two statements are critical in understanding the inherent aspects of the relationship between men and women.

"It is not good for man to be alone."

After having repeated seven times in chapter one that everything He had created was good, suddenly God tells us that one thing was not good. Was this an oversight on His part? No, it is stated this way for the purpose of emphasis. God had purposely created Adam with an inner emotional void that could not be satisfied completely by any other object that existed within the universe. It was a need that wasn't going to be met in the beauty of the creation, the pleasure of the garden with its luscious fruit and perfect climate, or in interacting with the myriads of exotic animals which surrounded him daily. There was only one creature who could fulfill this need: A Woman! Just as the soul of man is empty without God, the heart of man was empty without Woman. She was designed by God to be the perfect complement for that which was lacking in man.

"I will make a helper suitable for him."

The King James Version of the Bible translates this phrase

as a "help-meet." It sounds to our modern ears like an assistant or servant. Unfortunately, this has been the mistaken impression that has led at times to a denigrated view of women. The Hebrew (*'ezer*) does not imply a difference of value or status. It literally means "to help, aid, assist; as one succors the miserable and destitute."[9] What is a "succorer"? According to Webster, it is someone who provides "help, relief, aid, assistance; to help or relieve in need or difficulty."[10] It infers that the one helping possesses assets and/or abilities that the one needing help does not have. It is most frequently used in the Old Testament to describe the help or comfort we receive from the Lord in our times of need.

The principle of a succorer is expressed in Ecclesiastes 4:9-12:

Two are better than one, because they have a good return for their work: If one falls down, his friend can help him up. But pity the man who falls and has no-one to help him up! Also, if two lie down together, they will keep warm. But how can one keep warm alone? Though one may be overpowered, two can defend themselves.

Essentially, woman was given to be man's complement, counterpart and companion. There is a sense of partnership and mutual dependency. "Womankind" was created to bring to "mankind" something that was inherently lacking in the human community. The Amplified translation describes the woman as being one who is "suitable, adapted, completing." Without the woman, man was "alone," even though he was living in the midst of perfection.

"It is not good!"

Isn't it interesting that God is the one who declares, loneliness "is not good"? Loneliness is one of the most painful emotions in our lives. Every one of us have felt it, and we hate it. I believe this is what motivates us to turn on the TV or radio when we are alone, even when we aren't watching or listening. Somehow the noise helps us not feel so alone. Because we live increasingly isolated and lonely lives, we have searched for all sorts of substitutes for true companionship. I am convinced that the success of so many radio and TV talk shows is based on this reality.

Once I came across an advertisement in our local paper that stated, "Lonely?! I will talk about anything you want. $5 per call." As I understand it, this gentleman was making a great deal of money just listening non-critically to one caller after another. Why were they calling him? They didn't have anyone else to talk to.

One recent study revealed that this was especially true of men. They asked men and women the same question: "Do you have at least one other person you trust with your most intimate and personal issues?" Seven out of ten women said "Yes." Only one out of ten men could say the same. This becomes the basis of our search to find another person with whom we can share our lives—a partner, a companion, a fellow traveler through life.

Many years ago, a London newspaper ran an essay contest. The essay was to address in twenty-five words or less a simple question: What is the shortest route between London and Liverpool? Thousands sent in their responses. The winning essay? A single sentence: "The shortest distance between Liverpool and London is a good companion."

There is nothing that can better maximize the moments of our lives than good companionship. Good companionship is a function of intimacy and trust. We enjoy those with whom we feel safe. A good friend is someone who knows us intimately, warts and all, and still loves and respects us.

We have been essentially created as social beings. We need the interaction, the touch, the affection, the attention of other human beings, or we will die. How often children will misbehave because they are "just trying to get attention." God created us with a deep inner need for intimacy and ordained that its most perfect earthly fulfillment would be in marriage. This is the primary purpose of marriage!

Incompatible by design

When we fall in love, we focus on all the things we have in common and the things we like about our beloved. After marriage, we soon realize that, in many ways, we are very different from each other and there are things about our beloved that irritate us. Unfortunately, we usually do not realize God designed us to be essentially incompatible. That's right! Incompatible by design!

How boring it would have been if Eve would have been a clone of Adam. Instead, she brought into his life certain essential qualities and abilities that compensated for his areas of weakness. Like opposing cogs in a wheel, God's intent was to bring together these two different yet complementary beings who would be able to accomplish far more together than they could have ever done alone. This would be the key to productivity, creativity and emotional fulfillment.

How different are men and women?

There was a popular notion in the 1970s that men and women were essentially the same, aside from some very obvious anatomical differences. As is often the case, such ideas were not based upon scientific fact but upon a rather narrowly defined social agenda.

As any parent of opposite-sex children could tell you, there are profound differences between boys and girls. You can see it very early in life, and it becomes magnified as they grow older. One authority on human development recorded the following observations on the differences between baby boys and baby girls:

> Boy babies tend to cry more, sleep less, and smile less than girls. However, when confronted with stress, girls are more likely to cry, and boys are more likely to strike out in some way. Girls respond more positively to touch and sound and pictures of faces. Boys respond more positively to geometric designs. Girl babies tend to collect their treasures, their playthings and draw them close to themselves. Boys scatter them all over the room.

As we progress into adulthood, these differences become more specifically defined into differing orientations toward life in general. He goes on to note:

Men tend to be more interested in events, things, logic and the big picture. They are relatively less comfortable with, and sensitive to, the sharing of feelings. Their sexual expressions and feelings are more likely to be impulsive, reach a peak fast, be over fast, and be relatively less dependent upon the overall relationship.

Women are more tuned into people, to the details surrounding a person. . . . Relatively, women operate more on an intuitive feeling level. They tend to be more comfortable with expressions of feelings. Their sexual expressions are more likely to be an outgrowth of their overall relationship. The woman's more basic emotional need is to share meaningfully in another life.[11]

A 1988 US News and World Report article offered a comprehensive analysis of what scientists had concluded after years of study and research. They offered the following observations about the essential and inherent differences that exist between males and females, beginning at conception:

Birth

At birth the skeletons of girls are slightly more mature than those of boys. Girls are more responsive to touch and spend more time awake. Boys respond earlier to visual stimuli, girls to sounds and smells. Infant boys are far more likely than girls to be left-handed, nearsighted and dyslexic (more than 3 to 1). Males under 4 are also more likely than females to suffer from allergies and hiccups. Infant girls show a strong, early response to human faces—at a time when infant boys are just as likely to smile and coo at inanimate objects and blinking lights.

Toddler

By the end of the first year, boys gain and pass girls' skeletal maturity. At age 2, boys begin to show signs of greater aggressiveness. Girls have a slight edge in verbal skills, boys have greater spatial skills.

Adolescents

Girls begin to fall behind in body strength. The female superiority in verbal skills increases. So does the male edge in spatial skills and math.

Adult

The mature woman carries twice as much body fat as a man. The man carries 1 1/2 times as much muscle and bone.

Distinctive

Females have a better sense of smell. They are also more sensitive to loud sounds. Males are more sensitive to bright light—and can detect more subtle differences in light. Boys get more than 90 percent of all perfect scores of 800 on the math section of SAT's.

The authors go on to offer further commentary:

Differences appear as early as six weeks after conception ... There are differences between the sexes beyond their reproductive functions, the pitch of their voices, the curves of elbows and knees, the fecundity of hair follicles . . . Men's and women's brains are really different . . . in women, functions such as language ability appear to be more evenly divided between the left and right half of the brains; in men, they are much more localized in the left half . . . There are 13 male math geniuses for every female with such talent—and that the sex differences in math are the result of biological factors, perhaps exposure to the male sex hormone testosterone . . . Girls get better average grades in math at every level. Females are more attracted to people and males to objects . . . Boys have shorter attention spans. Boys and girls differ in their approach to moral problems . . . Girls see the moral problem in terms of "a narrative of relationships that extend over time." By contrast, boys see a "math problem." Men are more aggressive than women . . . If there is a feminine trait that's the counterpart of male aggressiveness, it's what social scientists awkwardly refer to as "nurturance." Women appear to be somewhat less competitive—or at least competitive in different ways than men. Men tend to be more "autocratic"—making decisions on their own —while women tend to consult colleagues and subordinates more often . . . Men will typically dominate the discussion . . . spending more time talking and less time listening.[12]

These observations are easy for all of us to identify with because they are so true. Why are men and women so different in how they think, feel and behave? Because God did not create Eve as a clone of Adam but as a "counterpart"! Women are supposed to be different from men. In many ways, men and women will never have a full understanding of each other. Their inherent differences in ways of looking and feeling about many things is too great to overcome. The challenge in marriage is to accept and respect those differences as part of the plan of God. It is God's will that we see the differences as an asset and not a threat. This is something we will be expanding on in a later chapter dealing with mutual respect.

"Bone of my bone and flesh of my flesh"

Herein lies the challenge. God not only created men and women to be different, He also created us to discover intimacy, in spite of our differences. Even though we are vastly different, we still have much more in common. There are more areas of our lives that overlap than conflict. This is especially true in the Christian marriage, where Paul reminds us that, "There is neither Jew nor Greek, slave nor free, male nor female, for you are all one in Christ Jesus" (Galatians 3:28). It is important to build upon those areas which we have in common and to learn to forbear those areas where conflicts are due to arise.

Adam quickly recognized that, although Eve was very different from him, she was also "bone of my bones and flesh of my flesh; she shall be called 'woman,' for she is taken out of man." His relationship with her would be so fulfilling, that it would be the impetus for a man to "leave his father and mother," and to form a new family.

I can only imagine the reaction of Adam as he awoke from his God-induced sleep. The operation being completed, looking slowly to his left, he sees her. She kind of looks like him, yet she is distinctly different—wonderfully different. I can almost hear him, jumping to his feet and shouting up to God, "Hey God, I don't know what it is, but I really, really like it!" But things were soon going to change. Adam was about to experience what we call Disillusionment!

4

Why Being Happily Married Is So Difficult

Then the eyes of both of them were opened, and they realized that they were naked; so they sewed fig leaves together and made coverings for themselves. Then the man and his wife heard the sound of the LORD God as he was walking in the garden in the cool of the day, and they hid from the LORD God among the trees of the garden. But the LORD God called to the man, "Where are you?" He answered, "I heard you in the garden, and I was afraid because I was naked; so I hid." And he said, "Who told you that you were naked? Have you eaten from the tree from which I commanded you not to eat?" The man said, "The woman you put here with me—she gave me some fruit from the tree, and I ate it." Then the LORD God said to the woman, "What is this you have done?" The woman said,"The serpent deceived me, and I ate" (Genesis 3:7-13).

Many couples I have talked to, without even realizing it have used a biblical phrase to describe the beginnings of disillusionment in their marriage: "and the eyes of both of them were opened." What is it that opened their eyes? The same thing that opens our eyes: One another's SIN!

Illusion!

Every marriage goes through three basic phases. The first is the Illusion Phase. This is the stage of romance and fantasy.

It is that wonderful frame of mind called infatuation. Unfortunately, it only lasts from two to four years. This is our favorite
time in a relationship. Studies have shown that during this
period in a relationship our sense of personal satisfaction is at
its highest. It's almost like being drugged. Our every thought
is upon the beloved. We can see no wrong in them; and if we
do, we are quick to overlook or excuse it.

Disillusion!

Somewhere between the second and fourth year of a relationship, the narcotic of infatuation begins to wear off. We begin to see our beloved with increasing objectivity. This is the
onset of the second stage in a relationship called the Disillusionment Phase.

How hard this phase hits us is largely dependent upon how
deeply infatuated we have been. The further our concept of
our beloved is from who they really are, the more dramatic the
drop-off from infatuation into the pit of reality. In the same
way the seriousness of jumping off a building is directly pro-
portionate to the height from which we jump, the higher we
are into our illusions about our beloved, the more devastating
it is when we realize that they are still part of the human race,
body odor and all.

This is the primary reason teenage marriages have such a
high failure rate. Age enables us to develop a more realistic,
even skeptical, view of our fellow man. We realize that there is
"no free lunch," "that things are not always what they appear!"
As we date different people, we learn that "there is more than
one fish in the sea," and that "all that glitters is not gold." We
have a term for this. It's called "growing up."

For my wife and me, our illusion was based upon our both
being Christians. We assumed that gave us an automatic ex-
emption from the kinds of problems and stresses we observed
other couples going through. Boy, were we wrong. What a
shock it was to discover we were both very self-centered and
self-protective.

Because of our experience, we slowly began to realize that
being a Christian didn't mean we were exempt from the
struggles, failures and suffering that the rest of humanity en-

counters. Rather, being a Christian gives the power and the perspective to "endure hardness as a good soldier of Jesus Christ" (2 Timothy 2:3).

Eve and the serpent

In Genesis 3, we see the beginnings of marital problems for Adam and Eve. It comes as a result of SIN! Often at this point we digress into theological discussions over who was more responsible for their sin, Adam or Eve. In the final analysis, they both were.

What is more important for us to recognize is "why" Eve gave in to the serpent's seduction. It is the same reason you and I give into doing, saying, thinking and speaking those things we know are wrong, committing what the Bible describes as willful disobedience.

Simply put, the serpent convinced Eve that it was more profitable to disobey than to obey God! That is the same reason you and I disobey. We decide that the cost of obedience is too high, too risky, too difficult, and we choose instead what appears to be the more comfortable, convenient, and/or advantageous path. We opt for immediate gratification over truth.

The serpent presented the temptation in terms that made sense to Eve's humanity: First he convinced her that God was holding out on her. "He doesn't want you to be just like Him and to have all the good things that He has." Secondly, he persuaded Eve that God could not be trusted and that His Word was not reliable. "You have eyes. You can see for yourself that the fruit is 'good for food,' and therefore should be eaten. It's also 'desirable for gaining wisdom,' and everybody can use more wisdom."

There was one thing the serpent said that was half true: "For God knows that when you eat of it your eyes will be opened, and you will be like God, knowing good and evil" (Genesis 3:5). This is the famous half-truth. It would be like me telling you, "If you jump off the Empire State Building, you won't be hurt." That's absolutely true. The jumping part would be completely painless. But when your body made contact with the pavement, you would look and feel like road-kill.

Once Adam and Eve ate of the fruit, they did become like God in one regard. Now their eyes were open and they knew the difference between "good and evil." Unfortunately, they lacked the ability to consistently do the good and, worse yet, the ability to resist the evil! Just knowing the difference between good and evil is no advantage. Knowing the difference does not empower you to do good or resist evil.

When we speak of sin, most of us think of it only in abstract terms: Other people's sin. We identify it with street crime, corporate and government corruption, Adolph Hitler, Josef Stalin, Idi Amin and Saddam Hussein. We can even see it in the guy who cut us off in traffic. But that isn't where sin has its most notable impact. Sin does its most obvious and immediate work in how we relate to and treat one another. If you want to know what's wrong with your marriage, it's sin—your sin! To prove my point, let's take a look at how it changed Adam's and Eve's relationship. What we will see is a downward progression from guilt, to shame, to compensation, to withdrawal and finally to self-justification.

The fact of guilt

Previously, we read, "The man and his wife were both naked, and they felt no shame" (Genesis 2:25). But following their sin, we read, "Then the eyes of both of them were opened, and they realized that they were naked" (Genesis 3:7). The immediate consequence of sin was "guilt," as their eyes were opened —opened to their disobedience and what it represented; opened to the great gap, morally and spiritually that now existed between them and God. Henceforth, it is the same for all who come into this world: "Therefore, just as sin entered the world through one man, and death through sin, and in this way death came to all men, because all sinned" (Romans 5:12).

What is guilt? It is the awareness that you are in the wrong, that you have committed an offense and are deserving of punishment. In that moment when "the eyes of both of them were opened," there was such a significant difference in their perceptions of everything. They became critically self-aware. They were faced with the fact of their guilt through sin. This was not just an emotional response. It began with reality of sin: "for all have sinned and fall short of the glory of God" (Romans 3:23). Fellowship with God had been broken!

The emotion of shame

What follows the "fact" of guilt is the emotion of shame! Suddenly we read that Adam and Eve are aware of their nakedness. It may be that their awareness was of both their spiritual as well as their physical nakedness.

Most of us do not realize that sin is what creates the feelings of shame—feelings that we all carry. Every one of us have "skeletons in the closet" that we would prefer no one ever finds out about. We all feel inadequate or incompetent about something. Women feel ugly; men feel unsuccessful. We become ashamed of how our lives have turned out or have failed to turn out. We may even struggle with "sins" of our past, transgressions that have scared and stained our memories. This terrible, haunting shame is the result of sin.

Efforts at compensation

So how did they react to their shame? Like all of us do when we are ashamed, they tried to cover it up: "so they sewed fig leaves together and made coverings for themselves" (Genesis 3:7). With fig leaves!? Yuk!

Have you ever picked figs? If you ever do, it is advisable to wear gloves, long-sleeve shirts and pants. Why? Because the juice will stain your skin, and the fibers from the leaves will make you itch. Can you imagine using fig leaves to cover your private parts? It could only make their nakedness more evident, and very uncomfortable.

That is always the effect of "cover-ups." They tend to aggravate the problem, making it more evident to others rather than less. Like the man who feels inadequate and therefore attempts to cover it up with braggadocio, or the woman who spends a fortune on clothes, cosmetic surgery, etc., seeking to mask the normal effects of aging. We develop a variety of compensators early in life when we become aware of our inadequacies and flaws. We may lie about our parents' occupations or income to impress our classmates. We may cheat or steal to have things that in our eyes make others significant. As time goes on, these behaviors become the very things that separate us from others and from God. We may live in daily, even hourly, fear that people will discover who we really are and reject us. Intimacy becomes impossible. We begin to build walls of separation to protect ourselves—walls that make it impossible for us to be open, honest and vulnerable with those we love. We find ourselves craving for intimacy but unable to "let down" our guard long enough to attain it.

When I was twelve years old, my parents had braces put on my extremely crooked teeth. This was a terrible fate for an insecure junior high student. I soon developed a compensator for my self-consciousness over wearing braces. Whenever I smiled, I would put my hand over my mouth so that no one could see my braces. Years later, long after my braces had been removed, someone asked me unexpectedly, "You used to wear braces didn't you?" When I asked how they knew, they told me they could tell by the way I covered my mouth whenever I smiled or laughed.

In many ways, that's what happens to us emotionally as well. We become so afraid of being vulnerable that we develop relational techniques that hinder our ability to become intimate with anyone, especially our spouse. We do it to protect ourselves from the shame we fear we will receive if we let the walls down and tell all. The problems with walls is that they not only protect, they imprison.

Remember, God said, "It is not good for man to be alone." But that is exactly what sin does to us. It has made us alone through our fear of being vulnerable. It made intimacy threatening, something to be feared. As a consequence, most of us have been lonely ever since.

The next verse tells, "Then the man and his wife heard the sound of the LORD God as he was walking in the garden in the cool of the day, and they hid from the LORD God among the trees of the garden" (Genesis 3:8). Not only did they become cut off from one another, they also became cut off from God!

I believe that there are two things that are absolutely essential for mental health: 1. Intimacy with God, and 2. Intimacy with others—so reads Proverbs 19:22, "What a man desires is unfailing love". The more comfortable we become with being honest with God and others about who we really are, the happier we will be.

Withdrawal from people and God

Sooner or later, the truth does come out. This is the fourth consequence of Adam and Eve's sin: "I was afraid because I was naked; so I hid" (Genesis 3:10). We become haunted by the fear of exposure. "What if people find out that . . . ?" What are they going to find out, that you are just like them? Somehow, we assume that we are the only one with our particular weakness or problem. I have found that that is always untrue.

Some years ago, I met regularly every Friday morning with a group of ten or twelve men for breakfast and fellowship. On one particular morning, the conversation drifted on to a hot topic in our community. A former Catholic priest was attempting to open a chain of pornographic shops around our city. Of course, all who were there were strongly against pornography and were very verbal in their opposition.

But then something wonderful happened. One of the men interrupted the conversation and said, "Men, I have a real problem with pornography. I know it's wrong, but I just can't stay away from it."

What followed was powerful. One by one, almost every man in that room began to share that he too struggled with pornography. For the first time, those men began to get real with one another. Fellowship began to really happen as we got honest. Ministry began taking place as men prayed for one another. For most of those men, it was the first time in their lives they had ever shared with another person on that level of honesty.

This is the kind of openness God intended to take place in marriage. Over the years, I have learned to share my deepest fears, struggles, guilt and shame with my wife. In the beginning, it was frightening. How would she react? Would she reject and disrespect me? Would she tell others?

How wonderful it has been as she has listened. She has comforted me, challenged me, counseled me; and on some occasions she has rebuked me because that is what I have needed. It has been at those times that I have most appreciated her role as my "counterpart."

Self-justification

Unfortunately, there have also been those times when I have not been so receptive to my wife's words. This is especially true when she is the one who initiates the discussion, usually discussions about my poor performance in one area or another. It's at those times that I see my behavior like that of Adam's and Eve's, when God confronts them in the Garden after they had sinned.

> And he said, "Who told you that you were naked? Have you eaten from the tree from which I commanded you not to eat?" The man said, "The woman you put here with me— she gave me some fruit from the tree, and I ate it." Then the LORD God said to the woman, "What is this you have done?" The woman said, "The serpent deceived me, and I ate" (Genesis 3:11-13).

What we see in this passage is the classic example of self-justification. Counselors refer to it as projection: The act of projecting the blame or responsibility for our actions upon someone else, thereby hoping to absolve ourselves from guilt and responsibility.

Adam and Eve's response to God's confrontation is almost as humorous as it is tragic. Adam doesn't even respond to God's question, "Who told you you were naked?" Instead he immediately begins to assign blame to Eve and God: "The woman you put here with me. . . ." Apparently following her husband's bad example, Eve follows suit: "The serpent deceived me, and I ate."

Everything they said was true, but it omitted one critical element: personal responsibility. Eve did not force Adam to eat of the fruit, neither did the serpent force Eve. They may have been coaxed, encouraged, seduced, deceived, but in the final analysis, it was their choice, through the exercise of their free will. They alone were guilty, and the judgment that followed was consistent with that fact.

I hate to admit it, but the above interaction between Adam, Eve and God sounds an awful lot like the way most of my "discussions" with my wife begin. When we point out failings in one another, rarely is it welcomed. I know what the Bible says: "Do not rebuke a mocker or he will hate you; rebuke a wise man and he will love you" (Proverbs 9:8). Unfortunately, I behave more like a "mocker" than a wise man. But this is an area where my wife has been one of my greatest assets.

Recently, my wife and I were shopping in a department store. As we were walking through the store, she turned to me and said, "Look at yourself in that mirror." Being an obedient husband, and having always enjoyed looking at myself in the mirror, I followed her command. To my embarrassment, I had a scowl on my face that was rather unattractive. It made it very evident that I was not having a good time. I immediately changed my expression and made a point to smile at everyone I encountered from that point on.

Why did my wife take the time to point out how unattractive I looked? Two reasons: One, she loves me and cares about how people view me. And two, she has to be seen with me in public. It was in both our best interests for me to be confronted and to change.

We must understand that God and others confront us most often for our own benefit, not to hurt us. Because we are sinners by nature and deed, the need for confrontation is frequent. It is also painful, as our "nakedness" becomes evident to others. But this is also the path to freedom, change and intimacy. Consider the words of Jesus in John 9, after he had healed the blind man:

> Jesus said, "For judgment I have come into this world, so that the blind will see and those who see will become blind." Some Pharisees who were with him heard him say this and asked, "What? Are we blind too?" Jesus said, "If you were blind, you would not be guilty of sin; but now that you claim you can see, your guilt remains" (John 9:39-41).

What are the "blind" spots in your life? Have you relied upon compensators, withdrawal or self-justifications to distance yourself from the problem areas in your life? Your marriage?

For my wife and me, the road to healing began when we no longer hid behind our accusations and blaming of one another. When we began to pray, "Lord show me where I have been at fault! Show me what I can do to change, to be a better husband, wife, father, mother," that's when real progress began to take place, for that was when we began to allow the Holy Spirit to change us!

> Humble yourselves before the Lord, and he will lift you up (James 4:10).

5

God's Ideal For Marriage

Submit to one another out of reverence for Christ. Wives, submit to your husbands as to the Lord. For the husband is the head of the wife as Christ is the head of the church, his body, of which he is the Saviour. Now as the church submits to Christ, so also wives should submit to their husbands in everything (Ephesians 5:21-24).

Most Americans are poor students of history and therefore lack historical perspective on the events that affect their lives. We tend to assume that the way things are today is the way they have always been. So when we talk about marriage, we assume that all peoples, in all times, had the same view that we have today. That is not the case.

When Paul wrote to the Ephesian church and outlined for them the attitudes and behavior that should govern marriage, he was writing something that was revolutionary to his time. He was confronting his first century readers with a view of marriage that was undoubtedly viewed as radical. It was a call for men and women to mutually submit to one another and serve one another in love.

Marriage to the first century Jew

To understand how radical this approach to marriage was, we need to understand the view of women and marriage that was common in the various dominant cultures in the first century. Let us begin by looking at Israel, for their attitude of women and marriage was much higher than that of the nations of the Gentiles.

Jewish women had far more status and security in a Jewish marriage because the Law condemned adultery and required a "writ of divorcement" if a man were to dispose of his wife. Even Solomon had counseled men to "rejoice in the wife of your youth" (Proverbs 5:18) and not to go seeking one younger and more attractive. The rabbis taught, "Every Jew must surrender his life rather than commit idolatry, murder, or adultery"; and "The very altar sheds tears when a man divorces the wife of his youth."

Yet, every Jewish man was instructed to begin his day with prayer, and that prayer included the following statement: "Thank you, O Lord, for not making me a Gentile, a slave or a woman." Women were often viewed not as people with status and position but as possessions, property.

One of the hottest topics of debate among the rabbis was the allowable grounds for divorcing a wife. There were essentially two schools of thought, each supported by highly respected rabbis. The conservative position was held by the followers of Hillel. They expressed his views this way: "A man might divorce his wife if she spoiled his dinner by putting too much salt in his food, if she walked in public with her head uncovered, if she talked with men in the streets, if she spoke disrespectfully of her husband's parents in her husband's hearing, if she was a brawling woman, if she was troublesome or quarrelsome." One of his supporters even went further: "A husband might divorce his wife if he found a woman whom he considered more attractive."[13]

Shammai, another respected teacher, held what was considered the more liberal position, stating that divorce was only allowable when the wife had committed adultery. It was into this controversy that the Pharisees sought to draw Jesus when they asked Him, "Is it lawful for a man to divorce his wife for any and every reason?" Jesus' response made it very clear what God's position was:

"Haven't you read," he replied, "that at the beginning the Creator 'made them male and female,' and said, 'For this reason a man will leave his father and mother and be united to his wife, and the two will become one flesh'? So they are no longer two, but one. Therefore what God has joined together, let man not separate." "Why then," they asked, "did Moses command that a man give his wife a certificate of divorce and send her away?" Jesus replied, "Moses permitted you to divorce your wives because your hearts were hard. But it was not this way from the beginning. I tell you that anyone who divorces his wife, except for marital unfaithfulness, and marries another woman commits adultery" (Matthew 19:4-9).

It appears that Jesus sided with the school of Shammai, (or Shammai sided with God!).

It is almost humorous to read the reaction of the disciples as they heard Jesus' response: "The disciples said to him, 'If this is the situation between a husband and wife, it is better not to marry'" (Matthew 19:10).

Marriage among the Greeks

The Jews were quick to decry the low morals of the Greeks, and rightly so. Consider the low view they held of women as illustrated through the comments of some of ancient Greece's greatest teachers.

Demosthenes, the greatest orator of ancient Greece, expressed the common view of his day this way: "We have courtesans for the sake of pleasure; we have concubines for the sake of daily co-habitation; we have wives for the purpose of having children legitimately and of having a faithful guardian for all our household affairs."

The Greek poet, philosopher and religious leader, Xenophon, summarized that the role of the wife was to "see as little as possible, hear as little as possible and ask as little as possible."

Even Socrates, who more than any other Greek philosopher profoundly affected Western thought, wrote regarding women, "Is there anyone to whom we entrust more serious matters than to your wife —and is there anyone to whom you talk less?" So much for the enlightenment of Greek thought!

Then there were the Romans

Without question, the lowest view of women and marriage existed among the Romans. By the first century, multiple marriages and divorces were common. As Gibbons noted, it was this more than anything else that brought on the eventual decline and collapse of the great Roman Empire.

It was against this cultural backdrop that Paul's words to the Ephesians was presented—in, of all places, the church located in the city of Ephesus, with its grand temple dedicated to the goddess Artemis (Diana, KJV)! She was the patroness of ceremonial prostitution, which was part of her worship at Ephesus. Her worship was characterized by sensuous orgies. Multitudes of female temple slaves or "priestesses," who came as virgins, were dedicated to service in the temple, which included ritual prostitution.

Here it is that Paul lays out the divine plan for marriage, one characterized by mutual love and sacrificial service. How wonderful the words of Paul must have sounded to the women of Ephesus as they saw the contrast of their own decadent culture, one which had reduced women to objects of pleasure. Now God had declared, "Husbands, love your wives, just as Christ loved the church and gave himself up for her to make her holy, cleansing her by the washing with water through the word, and to present her to himself as a radiant church, without stain or wrinkle or any other blemish, but holy and blameless." Here was the heart of God revealed!

Mutual submission

My father was not a Christian until a year and a half before his death. Yet, I remember him citing Ephesians 5:22-24 to my mother: "Wives, submit to your husbands as to the Lord. For the husband is the head of the wife as Christ is the head of the church, His body, of which He is the Saviour. Now as the church submits to Christ, so also wives should submit to their husbands in everything." His error was that he failed to consider this teaching in its greater context. Unfortunately, he was not alone in that error. It is not uncommon for husbands and wives to use this beautiful explanation of the ideal marriage as a weapon against their spouse. We are so good at telling others what they ought to do, while overlooking our own responsibilities.

Studies in context

To understand Paul's words, you need to examine them in the context in which they were given. Beginning in chapter four, Paul began outlining the practical application of our "position" as believers in Christ. Previously in chapter two, he declared that all who had believed in Christ were now "seated" with Christ "in the heavenly realm." This is how God views us. It is our "position" in Christ!

When he comes to chapter four, he follows with this exhortation: "As a prisoner for the Lord, then, I urge you to live a life worthy of the calling you have received" (Ephesians 4:1). What does "living a life worthy of our calling" involve? Verse two tells us: "Be completely humble and gentle; be patient, bearing with one another in love" (Ephesians 4:2).

From this point on, Paul gives numerous examples and applications of this principle to our lives: Grow in maturity (4:11-16); live as children of light (4:17-29); be imitators of Christ (5:1-21); glorify God in your marriages (5:22-31); glorify God in the family (6:1-4); glorify God on the job (6:5-9); glorify God through spiritual vigilance (6:10-19). The objective was to teach and challenge us to live our "position" in our daily lives, rather than surrendering to our sinful "condition."

It is within this context that Paul spoke to them about their marital relationships. He actually begins by presenting an overriding principle in verse 5:21: "Submit to one another out of reverence for Christ". Here is the objective to be reached in marriage—not just wives submitting to husbands, or husbands loving wives—rather, two Christians, motivated individually by a desire to honor and glorify Christ and, therefore, out of obedience and reverence to Him, "submitting to one another."

What do you mean when you say "I love you"?

Once my wife asked me, "Why do you love me?" She was not very thrilled with my answer, at least not until I had an opportunity to explain what I meant. I told her, "I love you because that is God's will." To her, it sounded like I was saying, "I don't really feel love for you, but it's my duty to love you, so I'll fake it for God's sake."

That was not at all what I meant. I love my wife for a number of reasons. I find her attractive; I enjoy her companionship and her support; she has loved me when I was not very lovable; she's borne four children, and she still looks great. But all of those reasons are "conditional." What if she wasn't attractive? What if we weren't such good friends? What if we had nothing in common? What if we had never had children? Would I still love her? Yes, I would, for Christ's sake!

This was Paul's point. Love is not really love until it becomes the "in spite of" kind of love. The love that is not based upon "what you have done for me lately," or what I hope you will do for me someday in the future. It is the love that has chosen to walk in love, to submit to and serve another, because it honors God.

Covenant vs. contract

This is why we refer to marriage as a "covenant" rather than a "contract." A contract is an agreement between two parties for the mutual exchange of goods and services. If, at any time, you fail to deliver on your part of the contract, I am free to dissolve the contract. This is the view most people today have of marriage. But God has called us into a covenant relationship that includes not just a man and a woman but also God. When we pronounce our marriage vows, in reality it is a man vowing to obey all that God commands of him regarding his wife. Likewise, the woman is committing to be faithful to God, in keeping all that He requires of her toward her husband. Our motive for loving one another is not based on the other's performance. Rather it is out of obedience to Christ.

I know this doesn't sound very romantic, but believe it or

not, this is the only basis upon which romance can last past the infatuation phase. There have been many times when I did not feel very loving or forgiving toward my wife. She may have hurt my feelings or disappointed me in some way. And yet, as I prayed about it, it always became clear what I was supposed to do: Love her for Christ's sake! Because romance is dependent upon confidence and trust, it is the consistency of our loving behavior that keeps the flames of romance alive.

I observed years ago that every Christian marriage would dramatically improve if Christians simply treated their spouses the way Jesus tells us we should treat our enemies. Compare what Jesus says to the way you treat your spouse: "But I tell you: Love your enemies and pray for those who persecute you," (Matthew 5:44). It is "love" that characterizes both the nature of God (1 John 4:16) and the primary evidence of a "spirit-filled" life (Galatians 5:22). If we are sincere in our desires to live lives "worthy of our calling", we must get serious about "loving one another" in marriage.

What kind of love?

Our language is far more limited in its expression and emphasis than the language of the Bible. Among the Greeks (which is the language of the New Testament), there were four different words that were used to describe different kinds of love:

1. There was the love of natural affection (*storge*), such as a parent would have for a child, or a patriot toward the nation of his origins.
2. There was covetous love (*eros*), which was often associated with sensual love.
3. There was the love of friendship (*philia*).
4. And lastly, there was the altruistic love (*agape*).

It is this last form of love that is most often associated with God's love for mankind and the love which Christians are called to show to others. This is the love Paul tells the Ephesians they are to show to one another, especially in the context of marriage (1:4; 2:4; 3:17,19; 4:16; 5:2,28; 6:23,24).

The best definition of agape love I have ever come across

was that written by W.E. Vine, in his *Expository Dictionary of New Testament Words*:

> Love can be known only from the actions it prompts. God's love is seen in the gift of His Son, 1 John 4:9,10. But obviously this is not the love of complacency, or affection, that is, it was not drawn out by any excellency in its objects, Romans 5:8. It was an exercise of the Divine will in deliberate choice, made without assignable cause save that which lies in the nature of God Himself, cp. Deut. 7:7,8.
>
> Love had its perfect expression among men in the Lord Jesus Christ, 2 Cor. 5:14; Eph 2:4; 3:19; 5:2. Christian love is the fruit of His Spirit in the Christian, Gal. 5:22.
>
> Christian love has God for its primary object, and expresses itself first of all in implicit obedience to His commandments, John 14:15,21,23; 15:10; 1 John 2:5; 5:3; 2 John 6. Self-will, that is, self-pleasing, is the negation of love to God.
>
> Christian love, whether exercised toward the brethren, or toward men generally, is not an impulse from the feelings, it does not always run with the natural inclinations, nor does it spend itself only upon those for whom some affinity is discovered. Love seeks the welfare of all, Rom. 15:2, and works no ill to any, 13:8-10; love seeks opportunity to do good to "all men, and especially toward them that are of the household of the faith," Galatians 6:10.[14]

Note the characteristics of Christian love:

1. "Love can be known only from the actions it prompts."
2. "It was not drawn out by any excellency in its objects."
3. "It was made without assignable cause."
4. "It expresses itself first of all in implicit obedience to His commandments."
5. "Self-will, that is, self-pleasing, is the negation of love to God."
6. "It is not an impulse from the feelings, it does not always run with the natural inclinations, nor does it spend itself only upon those for whom some affinity is discovered. Love seeks the welfare of all."

How does this compare to the way you treat the members of your household? If you are a Christian, this is not an option.

This is the command of God. Love is the most identifiable teaching found in the Bible. It is to be our most identifiable behavioral characteristic as Christians. It takes no great intellectual ability to comprehend what it is or what we are supposed to do. Yet, it is the most neglected part of the Christian life. We have become adept at explaining away why we aren't required to love some people or rationalizing loveless behavior as actually being love. If marriage is going to meet God's ideal, we must take seriously the responsibility to walk in unconditional love to one another, especially to those who are of the "household of faith"!

The "Loving" challenge to women

Someone once said that "Men marry women hoping they will never change, and women marry men hoping they will change." I do agree that most women marry men they mistakenly believe are everything they want them to be or they will be able to mold them into the man of their dreams. Neither is realistic, nor achievable.

Paul began his instructions on marriage by speaking to the wives. It is significant that he took three times as much space to speak to the men as he did to the women. Yet, it is his counsel to women that draws the most attention, primarily because of his instruction to "submit" to their husbands.

Paul based this counsel upon the principle of delegated authority. God has ordained that mankind live under the authority of three institutions: The Family, the Government, and the Church. The role of family is to train children "in the training and instruction of the Lord" (Ephesians 6:4). It is within the family that each of us learns to become civilized and socialized. The role of government is primarily to restrain evil by bringing "punishment of the wrongdoer" (Romans 13:4). Lastly, the role of the church is to proclaim the Gospel and to uphold the standard of righteousness. Within each of these institutions, there is a chain of authority, necessarily given if the role of each is to be adequately fulfilled.

Within the family, God has ordained that the man be the head of the family: "Now I want you to realize that the head of every man is Christ, and the head of the woman is man, and the head of Christ is God" (1 Corinthians 11:3). I recognize in today's world such a view sounds archaic, even oppressive. I have often had people cite the cases of abusive husbands and how wrong it is to tell women to submit to such men. For the record, this is neither what Paul nor I am saying. You must note that the principle of "headship" is predicated on the man having Christ as his "head." Abuse is obviously a sinful behavior, as well as a criminal one. God is not calling on women to submit themselves to criminal violence. What He is saying is that under normal and usual circumstances the family will reach its greatest benefit if the wife will acknowledge and support her husband's leadership in the home.

My experience has shown me that the far greater problem in families is not abuse but male abdication of leadership responsibilities. Too many men have become timid, reticent and/or too self-centered regarding their leadership roles. And too many women have been afraid to entrust that responsibility to their husbands. What we are dealing with here is not so much a control issue as it is a trust issue. Paul's statement to the wives is that they are to submit to their husband's authority, "as to the Lord." It is "to" the Lord, for the Lord's sake, if for no other reason.

I have had many women tell me that they couldn't trust their husbands to lead their families. I agree that there are some very immature and irresponsible men who are unreliable. But my question to these wives is, "What are you doing to help him become more responsible? Is your response feeding his immaturity by you taking all the burden upon yourself? Have you just taken the place of his mother?"

In such situations, there needs to be a strategy for change. It should begin with consistent prayer for God to set your home into its proper order. The wife needs to ask God to begin working in her heart, to help her remove attitudes and fears which may be contributing to her husband's abdication. It also requires a combination of encouragement and accountability. If a wife is constantly pointing out her husband's failings, she will only harden her husband's heart and close his ears to her words.

Ladies, can we talk for just a moment? Your husband needs to feel that you respect him. Granted, he may not have done the things that are important to you for you to feel respect for him. Therefore, you need to begin by "choosing" to respect him because God has put him into the position of leadership. We do this all the time in other areas of our lives. If the President of the United States were coming to your house for dinner, wouldn't you put out your best china and silver? You may not have even voted for the man. You may think his policies stink. But you would still show him the respect due his office. Why? Because it is right, and because the Bible commands it (Romans 13:1). We all realize that, no matter how poor a leader he may be, we must retain respect for the office if we are to maintain stability within the nation.

The family is no different. If we are to maintain the stability and dignity of the family, we must retain respect for the role of husbands and fathers. Your attitude and actions should be for the purpose of "building up" your house, not tearing it down. When you begin to do what is right, for the Lord's sake, God will in turn honor you. That is what the Bible repeatedly promises:

> Wives, in the same way be submissive to your husbands so that, if any of them do not believe the word, they may be won over without words by the behavior of their wives, when they see the purity and reverence of your lives (1 Peter 3:1,2).

Conversely, when a wife tears down her husband (especially before her children), she is destroying the very foundation upon which her authority and the respect of her children rests.

There is a wonderful relational principle that Jesus taught us in the Sermon on the Mount:

> Why do you look at the speck of sawdust in your brother's eye and pay no attention to the plank in your own eye? How can you say to your brother, "Let me take the speck out of your eye," when all the time there is a plank in your own eye? You hypocrite, first take the plank out of your own eye, and then you will see clearly to remove the speck from your brother's eye (Matthew 7:3-5).

Wives, does this sound like what you are doing? Are you rebelling against your husband's God-ordained role in your family? Did it ever occur to you, as you have been focusing on his failings (I'm sure you have a great deal of evidence to support your accusations), that you are overlooking a "plank" in your life?

Why should a woman submit to her husband? For the Lord's sake, for her sake, and for the sake of her children!

The wise woman builds her house, but with her own hands the foolish one tears hers down (Proverbs 14:1).

6

Lessons In Loving

Now as the church submits to Christ, so also wives should submit to their husbands in everything. Husbands, love your wives, just as Christ loved the church and gave himself up for her to make her holy, cleansing her by the washing with water through the word, and to present her to himself as a radiant church, without stain or wrinkle or any other blemish, but holy and blameless. In this same way, husbands ought to love their wives as their own bodies. He who loves his wife loves himself. After all, no-one ever hated his own body, but he feeds and cares for it, just as Christ does the church—for we are members of his body. 'For this reason a man will leave his father and mother and be united to his wife, and the two will become one flesh.' This is a profound mystery—but I am talking about Christ and the church. However, each one of you also must love his wife as he loves himself, and the wife must respect her husband (Ephesians 5:24-33).

Today, President Harry Truman is one of our most respected past national leaders. What most have admired about him was his "down to earth" approach to things. There was little evident pretense about the man. Regardless of what the job was, he knew what his responsibilities were, and he fulfilled them. On his desk in the Oval Office of the White House, he had a simple plaque that greeted everyone who entered there. It read, "THE BUCK STOPS HERE." Everyone who read it knew that President Truman was not going to shift the blame or waffle on a responsibility, and he wouldn't tolerate any staff or cabinet officer who did.

This nation needs more leaders with that kind of attitude today, not just in government, but at every level—men who live by their convictions and do it courageously, with a clear sense of right and wrong.

This is especially true in the home. Although men talk about women who won't submit, the far greater problem is men who won't lead. It is a particular kind of leadership that is needed. The theologians and preachers call it "servant-leadership," taken from the model and example that Jesus gave to His church. One of the best explanations of this leadership model was given by Jesus to His disciples, as they argued among themselves over who should be the greatest in Christ's coming kingdom. Listen to Jesus' response to their striving.

> Also a dispute arose among them as to which of them was considered to be greatest. Jesus said to them, "The kings of the Gentiles lord it over them; and those who exercise authority over them call themselves Benefactors. But you are not to be like that. Instead, the greatest among you should be like the youngest, and the one who rules like the one who serves. For who is greater, the one who is at the table or the one who serves? Is it not the one who is at the table? But I am among you as one who serves (Luke 22:24-27).

As males, this is where our greatest conflict begins. God is the exact opposite of how we have come to understand our roles in this world. Our heroes are the winners, the champions, the conquerors! Every man has a secret dream of greatness. Probably the main cause of mid-life crises is the feeling that "greatness" and significance have passed us by and we will be forever "ordinary." We dedicate so much of our energy trying to achieve "our" goal. Sometimes, it's not until we have climbed to the top of the ladder that we realize our ladder was leaning against the wrong wall.

The question for every man, especially every Christian man, is "Who's your audience of significance?" What audience are you seeking to please? Your peers? Your parents? Friends, associates, co-workers? When you have done your best, or when you have failed, whose reaction means the most to you? The correct answer should be God, because that is what the Bible teaches: "So whether you eat or drink or whatever you do, do it all for the glory of God" (1 Corinthians 10:31). It is to Him that we must give account for every moment of our lives. When we stand before His holy presence in eternity, all that will matter is how He views our works. In that day and hour, the words you and I will want to hear the most are "Well done thou good and faithful servant, . . . enter into the joy of the Lord" (Matthew 25:21, KJV).

It is logical, then, that if our greatest desire is to please Him with our lives, that will also be our dominant concern as husbands. In other words, I should seek to be as He was in every situation I face. As John put it, "Whoever claims to live in him must walk as Jesus did" (1 John 2:6).

What is the example with which He has left us? Paul, in Philippians 2 summarizes it best:

> Your attitude should be the same as that of Christ Jesus: Who, being in very nature God, did not consider equality with God something to be grasped, but made himself nothing, taking the very nature of a servant, being made in human likeness. And being found in appearance as a man, he humbled himself and became obedient to death—even death on a cross! Therefore God exalted him to the highest place and gave him the name that is above every name (Philippians 2:5-9).

According to Paul, Jesus' life was marked by four things:

1. "He made Himself nothing." (KJV reads "made Himself of no reputation.")
2. "He took the very nature of a servant."
3. "He humbled Himself."
4. "He became obedient to death."

And what was the consequence? "Therefore God exalted Him to the highest place . . . ." Herein is the key to living a life of significance! It does not come by building, climbing, amassing, striving, gaining, overcoming, etc.—all the things the world around us thinks makes for significance. Rather, if we become imitators of Christ, if we seek to be the kind of leader that He was, GOD WILL EXALT US!

Reflect for a moment on these four characteristics of Jesus, our leader. How does your attitude compare? If asked, would your wife and friends say this is a description of your character?

As my dear friend Stanley Voke once pointed out, long before Jesus became the Great Shepherd of our Souls, He first became the Lamb of God. And what are the qualities of lambs as they appear in the Old Testament? They were pure; they were humble; and they were bred for sacrifice! Jesus was a lamb in shepherd's clothing, not a wolf in sheep's clothing. And what does the Bible teach us regarding the life that Jesus lived? "To this you were called, because Christ suffered for you, leaving you an example, that you should follow in his steps" (1 Peter 2:21). And what were the "steps," or footprints, our Shepherd left for us to walk in? Simply, before we can become shepherds, we must first become lambs—lambs who are pure in our motives and manner; humble in heart; willing, committed to sacrifice ourselves for those whom Christ has committed to our oversight!

The greater challenge for husbands

For many years, the focus in marriage was primarily upon the role of the woman. Not so with the Bible. The Bible has much more to say about the man's responsibility than it does the woman's. Even in the Ephesians 5 passages we have been looking at, there are three times as many verses dealing with the man's responsibilities in the marriage than that of the woman. And what is stated there is far more compelling.

When Paul wanted to illustrate the role and responsibilities of men in marriage, he drew on the image of Christ and the church. His instructions are clear enough: "Husbands, love your wives, just as Christ loved the church and gave himself up for her" (Ephesians 5:25). It is the simplicity and clarity of what he is saying that makes us shy away from trying to follow it. How is it possible for me to love my wife "just" as Christ has loved the church?

When I tell you that this is the objective to be achieved,

understand that I doubt I have ever consistently lived at (or ever will) such a level of Christlikeness. That is because what Paul is stating here is the "ideal," the standard of perfection and excellence. Some, unfortunately, have used the impossibility of being perfect in this area as a reason not to try. Oftentimes, a wife contributes to the man's discouragement by reminding him that he is not loving her as Christ has loved the church. No matter how true this may be, I think it is unfair and counterproductive.

We are defined by our ideals as much as we are by our behavior. If I decide that being Christlike is impossible, and I choose an easier objective, I will fall short of that as well. The important thing to remember is that Christ will make up for our shortfall. He sees the intent of our hearts, and He grants to us the grace to accomplish His will. As Paul tells the Corinthians, "And God is able to make all grace abound to you, so that in all things at all times, having all that you need, you will abound in every good work" (2 Corinthians 9:8).

And what is God's will for you as a husband? To love your wife as He loves the church! This becomes the focus of his comments that follow. We could summarize his instructions as defining five different kinds of love: sacrificial (5:25), purifying (5:26,27), caring (5:28-30), unbreakable (5:31), and God-reflecting love (5:32)!

Sacrificial love

Husbands, love your wives, just as Christ loved the church and gave himself up for her (Ephesians 5:25).

Paul begins his loving instructions to husbands, telling them that love must be of the same kind that Jesus showed when He "loved the church and gave Himself up for her." There are many ways we can explain love and many different levels on which it can operate, but there is only one ultimate and ideal definition of love: "For God so loved the world that He gave His one and only Son, that whoever believes in Him shall not perish but have eternal life" (John 3:16).

Freely, unconditionally, sacrificially, God expressed His love for His church through His Son, Jesus. This love-act of God communicates two things to us:

1. It revealed and validated the true nature of God as "love" (1 John 4:8).

2. It clearly and concisely defined how the church individually and corporately is to treat others.

As John explains:

> This is how God showed his love among us: He sent his one and only Son into the world that we might live through him. This is love: not that we loved God, but that he loved us and sent his Son as an atoning sacrifice for our sins. Dear friends, since God so loved us, we also ought to love one another (1 John 4:9-11).

It is important to note, when Paul challenges husbands to love their wives, this should be obvious, for that is how we are to treat everyone, even our enemies! How much more our wives?!

Redefining love

What causes both men and women to stumble in this area is the way our culture increasingly chooses to define love. It's usually characterized by warm feelings, erotic passions, scintillating sensations, long and tender gazes, gentle touches, romantic dinners under candlelight, evenings alone in front of a warm fire at some remote mountain cabin. But this is not the picture the Bible draws for us. The love it speaks of is pictured first and foremost in the sweat and blood of our Savior as He struggles to carry the cross through the streets of Jerusalem. His face is bruised and broken, His back torn by the whip, with bone and muscle exposed. Here is love seen in its purest form, willingly submitting to the insults, mocking and jeering. As He is thrown to the ground so His arms can be bound to the transit and the spikes driven into His hands, we realize that all of this was for us . . . and because of us! He is hoisted up against the pole, the cross-bar is connected, and His feet are nailed to the pedestal. We can see the blood slowly trickling from His wounds. There He hangs, laboring under the burn, the ache, the throb, the piercing of ever-increasing and excruciating pain. Worse yet is the anguish of His heart, the agony of soul over the sin of those He loves.

It was at this moment that He looked down upon the soldiers below, only a few feet away. They are oblivious to His suffering, long ago calloused by their hatred for the Jews and the commonness of crucifixion duty; they are too absorbed in their greed to notice, to care about His sufferings. They are busy . . . gambling over His few earthly possessions, their reward for their sadistic labors. In this moment of supreme blasphemy and contradiction, the love of God is given vocal expression. To the amazement of those few who had followed Him to the cross, they suddenly heard Him utter a holy prayer, a prayer of utter selflessness: "Father, forgive them, for they do not know what they are doing" (Luke 23:34).

When we begin to see such events as being the truest and best definition of love, then we begin to approximate what Paul was referring to when he challenged you and me to love our wives "as Christ loved the church." In an instant, it banishes all of my excuses for not loving. I become ashamed as I am forced to see how petty my complaints and bitterness are in comparison to His sufferings. How wrong I begin to feel when I recall my harsh responses and critical comments, in light of how Jesus behaved upon the cross: "When they hurled their insults at Him, He did not retaliate; when He suffered, He made no threats. Instead, He entrusted Himself to Him who judges justly" (1 Peter 2:23).

"It's more blessed to give . . . but"

It is painful to admit that most of the time I pursue the wrong images of love. What is even more difficult is facing the real reason why I prefer a shallower way: I am basically selfish! You would think I would know better. Anyone can see how selfishness is a "love killer." It breeds such ugly things, like pride, greed, envy, jealousy, arrogance, and the like. It produces an approach to life I call "relational hedonism" that thinks only in terms of how I can get the maximum benefit for the minimum investment! Haven't we all learned that this is the wrong way to happiness? Didn't Jesus teach us that it is more "blessed to give than to receive"?

True love usually does not take very dramatic forms. It's helping my kids with their homework at the end of a long and hard day, even though I want to relax, watch TV, or go to sleep. It's helping my wife clean the house on my day off or turning off the ballgame so I can listen to her without distraction. It's listening to someone who is hurting or lonely, being patient with someone who is slow to learn or understand, forgiving someone who has slandered me or said something hurtful behind my back, or humbling myself by asking someone to forgive me for something I have done to hurt them.

This is the very thing which makes loving others so very hard. As Bill Hybels expressed it:

> Tell me that love can be demonstrated to other people without it costing me my time, my energy, my money, and I will gladly involve myself. Tell me what line to stand in, which project to sign up for, which person to commit myself to, and I'll join.
>
> But look me straight in the eye and tell me that love is synonymous with sacrifice, that loving someone is going to require that I part with my time, my energy and my resources, and I become very reluctant to commit myself; I don't want to sign dotted lines. I hesitate to volunteer or get involved.[15]

Let's face it men! If we are ever going to fulfill our roles as husbands, we must arm our minds with one concept: LOVE = SACRIFICE! True loving has more to do with work than play, serving than celebrating, giving than receiving. Often, true love hurts!

Purifying love

> Husbands, love your wives, just as Christ loved the church and gave Himself up for her to make her holy, cleansing her by the washing with water through the word, and to present her to Himself as a radiant church, without stain or wrinkle or any other blemish, but holy and blameless (Ephesians 5:25-27).

In Matthew 5, we have the beginning of the most famous sermon Jesus ever preached. We call it "The Sermon on the

Mount." It opens with the Beatitudes, or "principles for blessing." In the opening ten verses, Jesus lists nine behaviors that will lead to blessing. Have you ever asked the question, "Which of the Beatitudes is the most difficult to keep?" Can I suggest the one I think it would be? "Blessed are the pure in heart, for they will see God" (Matthew 5:8).

Purity is highly valued in both people and things. *Katharos* (Greek) originally was used to describe the purity of things—pure water, pure gold, etc. Over time, it came to refer to purity of motives: Motives free from corrupt desire, sin and guilt; free from every admixture of what is false; sincere, genuine, blameless, innocent, unstained with the guilt of anything.

It is from such motives that Paul tells a man to serve his wife, for these were Christ's motives. Paul presents Jesus' ministry to the church as follows:

1. "To make her holy."
2. "To cleanse her . . . through the word."
3. "To present her . . . holy and blameless."

These should be the desires of a true shepherd. His words and actions are calculated to "prepare God's people for works of service, so that the body of Christ may be built up until we all reach unity in the faith and in the knowledge of the Son of God and become mature, attaining to the whole measure of the fullness of Christ" (Ephesians 4:12,13). Seeing his wife mature in Christ is more important than any pleasure, comfort or benefit she might bring to his life. Therefore, he faithfully prays for her and with her. He studies the Word of God so he might understand the Word, so he can both live it and model it. He encourages her to grow in Christ through the example of his life. He never condemns her failings, nor does he ignore them. "Instead, speaking the truth in love, we will in all things grow up into him who is the Head, that is, Christ" (Ephesians 4:15).

Unfortunately, it is very easy for men to become impure in their motives toward their wives. It takes no effort to see her as a means to our own comfort and pleasure. To understand how displeasing this is to God, we need to look at the Old Testament books of Jeremiah and Ezekiel. God had placed the spiritual leaders of Israel over the nation, as a shepherd places under-shepherds over his sheep. But instead of caring for and protecting the flock of God, they used them to satisfy their own appetites. Listen to the indictment the Lord brings against them:

> Son of man, prophesy against the shepherds of Israel; prophesy and say to them: "This is what the Sovereign LORD says: Woe to the shepherds of Israel who only take care of themselves! Should not shepherds take care of the flock? You eat the curds, clothe yourselves with the wool and slaughter the choice animals, but you do not take care of the flock. You have not strengthened the weak or healed the sick or bound up the injured. You have not brought back the strays or searched for the lost. You have ruled them harshly and brutally" (Ezekiel 34:2-4).

In contrast to these unfaithful shepherds, Jeremiah tells us what role the shepherds were supposed to fulfill: "Then I will give you shepherds after my own heart, who will lead you with knowledge and understanding" (Jeremiah 3:15).

Men, take a moment to evaluate your role as the shepherd or pastor of your home. Have you shepherded after God's heart? Or have you been motivated by selfish desires? Is it time for you to humble yourself before the Lord and your wife, repenting and asking forgiveness?

Caring love

> In this same way, husbands ought to love their wives as their own bodies. He who loves his wife loves himself. After all, no-one ever hated his own body, but he feeds and cares for it, just as Christ does the church—for we are members of His body (Ephesians 5:28-30).

One of the most fascinating differences between men and women is revealed in how they feel about their bodies. No matter how beautiful a woman may be, she is never certain that she is beautiful. She requires constant reassurance. When she stands in front of a mirror, she usually sees herself in the worst possible light. She is either too short or too tall; her breasts are too small or too large; her eyes are too far apart or too close; her lips are too full or too thin. It goes on and on. You can pick any part of her body, any aspect of her anatomy, and she will tell you why it isn't perfect, and therefore, why it needs to be hidden, painted over, removed or reshaped.

Recently, my wife and I were shopping for a full-length mirror to put in our bathroom. After looking at several different kinds of mirrors, my wife finally settled upon one she liked. Then she asked me to hold it up while she stood at the far end of the aisle so she could look at herself. Being an ignorant male, I asked an obvious question: "Why do you want to look at yourself in the mirror?" "I want to buy one that makes me look thin," she replied. As a man, this would never have occurred to me. I would have reasoned, "If the mirror makes me look larger than I am, it's just a mirror, and I will always know it's a distortion." It would not have occurred to me to select one that puts my appearance in the best light. (As I was telling this story to someone, they informed me that if you tilt the mirror out from the bottom when you hang it, it will always make you look thinner. Come to think of it, it was a woman who shared this technique with me!)

On the other hand, men tend to give themselves the benefit of the doubt. We assume that we look better than the reflection in the mirror. For example, a man can be walking down the street and suddenly catch his reflection in a mirror or display window—he can have a beer-belly hanging several inches over his belt line—yet upon seeing himself, he will suck in his gut as far as possible and declare with satisfaction, "I still look pretty good!" I can't imagine a woman ever responding like that.

Paul couldn't have tagged it any better than when he said, "After all, no-one ever hated his own body, but he feeds and cares for it . . . ." This is probably true for both men and women, but it is especially true for men. We know that if we neglect our bodies they will not function well, or for long. That is why we "feed it and care for it."

Importantly, Paul adds this comment, "He who loves his wife, loves himself." This principle grows out of the fact of oneness. After marriage, a man and woman are one flesh. They no longer live separate, independent lives. What affects one, affects the other; what wounds or injures one, also touches the other. It is the same principle that applies to the church, for the family is, in reality, a microcosm of the church. Paul expresses it, "If one part suffers, every part suffers with it; if one part is honored, every part rejoices with it" (1 Corinthians 12:26; also Romans 12:25; Ephesians 4:25). Being "care-full" of my wife and her needs will return to me again. A wife's happiness is most often the means of her husband's happiness. There is nothing more crushing to the male ego than to know that he is the cause of his wife's unhappiness. That is why it is so hard for a man to take responsibility for those things that are hurtful to his wife.

What does it mean to be "caring"? I prefer the Authorized Version's rendering of this word. Instead of "cares," they used the word "cherisheth." I believe this is closer to the original, which means "to cherish and foster with tender love and care." One dictionary offers the following descriptive statements about what it means to "cherish" someone:

1. To view with an elevated feeling of pleasure.
2. To hold in high esteem.
3. To provide shelter or a refuge.
4. To feel a lover's passion, devotion or tenderness for.
5. To promote the growth, development or progress of.
6. To honor and admire profoundly and respectfully.
7. To supervise or take charge of.

Consider how similar this definition is to the Apostle Paul's description of his care for the churches as their pastor: ". . . but we were gentle among you, like a mother caring for her little children" (1 Thessalonians 2:7). Peter declares the manner in which God cherishes His church, by describing her as ". . . a chosen people, a royal priesthood, a holy nation, a people belonging to God, that you may declare the praises of him who called you out of darkness into his wonderful light. Once you were not a people, but now you are the people of God; once you had not received mercy, but now you have received mercy" (1 Peter 2:9,10). If we were to look for synonyms, we would use words like "tender-love, gentleness, admiration, appreciation, esteem, valuing."

It is important that we understand the importance of love that cherishes. Long ago, it was found that babies fail to thrive, and even die, without any other assignable cause, if they are deprived of tender affection. The loving touch, the warm embrace, the gentle kiss—all are vital parts of our survival.

One recent German study found that couples who kiss regularly on average lived longer. The researchers concluded that one of the healthiest things a married couple can do before leaving for work each morning is to embrace and kiss passionately. (When I shared this with my wife, she told me she would rather die young!)

Such finding shouldn't be such a surprise to us. It doesn't take a rocket scientist to recognize that "being loved" boosts one's morale. It is also a powerful motivator. Think of all the things that have been done, both good and bad, motivated solely by love for another. Parents, friends, spouses, children, have literally given all, even their lives, for someone they loved.

When Jackie DeShannon sang, "What the world needs now is love sweet love," she was hitting our emotional bullseye. Unfortunately, most men miss this target completely. In this age of Rambos, Terminators and Robocops, most men are concerned only with being tough, not tender. There is nothing wrong with being strong. But tenderness is also a sign of strength. In fact, for many men, this is a far greater challenge. For them, "toughness" has become a means of emotional protection. It sends out a message, "If you hurt me, I'll hurt you back." It creates an isolation which leaves the man's need for tenderness unmet. His inability to cherish others results in his own unfulfilled need to be cherished.

One of the more common complaints men offer regarding their wives is "nagging." Few have even considered that they may be a key contributor to their wive's nagging. Women often become naggers when they feel their husbands cannot be trusted to care for their needs. The best way to stop your wife's nagging is to become more sensitive to her needs, to become gentle and caring.

One of best passages for married couples to read together is found in Ephesians 4:29-5:2. Although Paul is writing to the whole church, and every Christian, it is especially applicable to husbands and wives.

Do not let any unwholesome talk come out of your mouths, but only what is helpful for building others up according to their needs, that it may benefit those who listen. And do not grieve the Holy Spirit of God, with whom you were sealed for the day of redemption. Get rid of all bitterness, rage and anger, brawling and slander, along with every form of malice. Be kind and compassionate to one another, forgiving each other, just as in Christ God forgave you. Be imitators of God, therefore, as dearly loved children, and live a life of love, just as Christ loved us and gave Himself up for us as a fragrant offering and sacrifice to God (Ephesians 4:29-5:2).

Unbreakable love

For this reason a man will leave his father and mother and be united to his wife, and the two will become one flesh (Ephesians 5:31).

Four times in the Bible we read the following statement: "For this reason a man will leave his father and mother and be united to his wife, and the two will become one flesh" (Genesis 2:24, Matthew 19:5; Mark 10:7; Ephesians 5:31). This was the first statement in the Bible explaining the fundamental basis of marriage. Thereafter, it became the reference point for all the biblical teachings on marriage, being quoted by both Jesus and Paul. It summarizes the behaviors that are essential for a marriage to survive: A man and a woman must be willing to "leave" behind all other primary relationships and to replace them with the new marital bond. This process of bonding is called "cleaving." It is cleaving that leads to a state of "oneness."

Leaving

This involves far more than one might realize, because it is a lifelong process, which we enter into rather unwillingly. That's because it requires us to leave the homes in which we grew up—the places where we learned and discovered most of what we know about ourselves, other people and the world around us. It's leaving a place of security, where you know all the rules and systems, everything and everyone is predictable. Additionally, the family is where our basic values, principles, goals—our entire concept of what is true and real—are instilled and developed.

It is also the place where our ways of doing things is learned. For example, my mom always filled the kitchen with dirty pots, pans, dishes and utensils when she cooked. When dinner was finished and conversation had ended, then she would clean up the mess. And by the way, she never expected the men to help out, because kitchen cleanup was women's duty. (Bless her soul!) In contrast, my mother-in-law would use a pot or pan, and when she was finished with it, she cleaned it and put it away. Her work surfaces were always neat, orderly and clean. She could only enjoy her dinner knowing that the work of cleanup was done.

Which way was right? Which was wrong? Neither! Yet one of the very first conflicts my wife and I had was over these kinds of issues. I was sure that my mother's way was the best, because it was what I knew and was comfortable with. She felt the same way about her mother's approach. We each viewed the other's tradition as being inefficient and impractical. It never occurred to us that we had the liberty to sit down and work out our own arrangement, that we were not bound to the ways of our parents, that we had a freedom to design our own approach to such things.

My father rarely did housework. My wife's father was always willing to help out. My father never took out the garbage; her father always did. When my wife requested my help with housework or taking out the garbage, I felt she was trying to usurp my role by getting me to do women's work. She, on the other hand, was hurt and angry because I was unwilling to fulfill the most basic of my husbandly responsibilities.

It took us several years to work through these kinds of conflicts. Only after we recognized that we were still living with our parents in our heads, that we were still "cleaving" to their ways and not setting up our own unique household, did we begin to experience "unity" in our living relationship.

Every family is part of the larger culture. At the same time, every family will have its own traditions which make it a unique culture within itself. In that sense, every marriage is a cross-cultural marriage. Most of us recognize how challenging it is to marry someone from a different country. The challenge may not be as great when you marry the girl or guy next door, but it will still be a challenge.

Never underestimate the force of your parents' culture upon your view of things. For most of us, they shaped our total view of the world for at least twelve years. When we hit our teens, we rebelled and determined that we weren't going to be like our parents; we were going to be different, to do things differently. And we can, if we begin by recognizing what things are worth keeping, what things are negotiable, and what things should be thrown out.

I am not saying that we don't gain valuable things from our upbringing. After all, the primary role of parent is to "Train a child in the way he should go, and when he is old he will not turn from it" (Proverbs 22:6). But this primarily refers to principles of faith and godly living. These are non-negotiable, absolute truths upon which life and reality rests. We err when we major on the minors—when we cling to things like who takes out the garbage or does the housework, as if they are the most important issues in our lives. Remember, the non-negotiables are the things which God has given us in His Word. I have never read anything in the Bible about who takes out the garbage or cleans the dishes. I have noticed frequent references to serving one another in love!

A military strategist once said, "Pick carefully the hilltop you want to die on!" In warfare, you can't hold every hilltop, and trying to do so may win you a lot of battles but cost you the war. The same holds true in marriage. Face the fact early on that staying married requires both husband and wife to give ground in various places. It helps to identify early the important things that are non-negotiable. Ideally, you identified these before marriage—like, are you both committed, mature Christians?! These non-negotiables become the basis upon which the relationship is built, not the cause of conflict. This is exactly what Paul was speaking about in 2 Corinthians 6:14: "Do not be yoked together with unbelievers. For what do righteousness and wickedness have in common? Or what fellowship can light have with darkness?"

Cleaving

The second part of becoming "one" requires a man and woman to "cleave" to one another. Significantly, the Greek word used here (*proskollao*) means "to glue together, to join one's self to another closely, cleave to, stick to." It refers to the closest and most inseparable bonds, like the layers of wood that make up a sheet of plywood, they are joined together to provide greater strength. If you were to attempt separating the various layers of the plywood, you would only destroy it. Have you ever attempted to separate two pieces of wood that have been glued together? You may succeed at separating them, but the line of separation will not be the same. Part of one piece will tear away, still connected to the other. That is what it is like when a divorce takes place. We may tear away and break free from our spouses, but part of them will always be with us. We cannot go back to the way we were before we married. We are forever changed . . . damaged!

Why is this? When a man and woman are wed, they are submitting themselves to a divine event that includes not them alone but also God. The minister who officiates the wedding service stands as a representative of God first and second as an agent of society. He is literally there in Christ's stead—a symbolic testimony that the union is being prescribed and validated before God, as well as man. The Bible teaches that it is God alone who "joins together." Divorce is essentially an undoing of the work of God, a retraction of what God has caused to be. That is why Jesus declared, "So they are no longer two, but one. Therefore what God has joined together, let man not separate" (Matthew 19:6).

The phrase "joined together" (*suzeugnumi*) means "to fasten to one yoke, or to yoke together." The picture is of two oxen which have been yoked together to pull a plow or cart. They are no longer two, but "one yoke of oxen." The yoke keeps them banded together. To separate them would be a sabotage to all their owner had purposed for them.

So also, when a man and woman are married, they have become "yoked together." They are no longer two, but one. To separate them is to sabotage the greater purposes of God for which their union was purposed. As we submit ourselves to

this "yoke," over time we increasingly discover the good purposes of God and the marvelous wonder of His ways. Truly,
two becomes "better than one."

This divine union is far more than a physical, sexual union,
although that is a part of it. Living in the same house, sharing
income and physical intimacy, does not make for oneness.
Oneness begins when we make an unconditional commitment
to our marriage partner. As we grow in that commitment, daily
facing its challenges, our sense of oneness grows. It is a life-
long process that improves with usage. The threat to oneness
most often begins with unresolved hostility. Paul writes, "Husbands, love your wives and do not be harsh with them"
(Colossians 3:19). The folly of bitterness easily can be seen when
we transfer it to the previous picture of the two oxen yoked
together. Think about it. Everything one ox might do to hurt
the other only causes himself suffering. If he wounds the other,
then he must carry both his load and hers. If he refuses to pull
his weight, the labor is slowed and the farmer (God, 1 Peter
3:7) will punish him. It clearly is in his own best interest to
seek unity with the one with whom God has yoked him.

God-reflecting love

> This is a profound mystery—but I am talking about
> Christ and the church (Ephesians 5:32).

When a couple is in conflict, it is very difficult for them to
view their relationship with objectivity. They are convinced
that if the other one will just stop doing the things which are
causing conflict their marriage would improve instantly. Of
course, when you have two people with this same perspective,
all that results is a tug-of-war of wills. Over time, they become
increasingly entrenched in their positions and opinions of one
another. The situation becomes like that described by the
Apostle Paul when he warned the Galatians, "If you keep on
biting and devouring each other, watch out or you will be destroyed by each other" (Galatians 5:15).

What is overlooked by most couples in this situation is the
essential purpose of marriage: to glorify God! In fact, this is
supposed to be the core of everything that happens in our lives.

When the Psalmist cried out for help from the Lord, he implored the Lord to "Help us, O God our Saviour, for the glory of Your name; deliver us and atone for our sins for Your name's sake" (Psalms 79:9). Paul exhorts that, "So whether you eat or drink or whatever you do, do it all for the glory of God" (1 Corinthians 10:31). Peter explains that, "If anyone speaks, he should do it as one speaking the very words of God. If anyone serves, he should do it with the strength God provides, so that in all things God may be praised through Jesus Christ. To Him be the glory and the power for ever and ever. Amen" (1 Peter 4:11).

I could go on and on with biblical references, all clearly affirming that the ultimate objective of the Christian life, in every area of our lives, is to glorify God. One of my elders, a successful businessman in our community, once expressed this concept to a group of men. He said, "Gentlemen, the purpose of business is to glorify God." Most of them, including me, had always thought that the purpose of business was to make money. But God had shown him something that had never occurred to the rest of us—something which makes complete sense and is totally logical, when considered in the light of God's revelation through His Word. Of course the purpose of business is to glorify God. John, in his Revelation, declares:

> Who will not fear you, O Lord, and bring glory to your name? For you alone are holy. All nations will come and worship before you, for your righteous acts have been revealed (Revelation 15:4).

When glorifying God becomes the driving motivation behind a business, God is freed to glorify Himself through that business and to bless the man who is the steward of that business. "Those who honor me I will honor, but those who despise me will be disdained" (1 Samuel 2:30).

In like manner, this principle applies to marriage and every other area of our lives. God wants to extend His kingdom, His lordship, to every area of our lives. This is a life-long process, as God daily takes new ground in our lives. Is it surprising, therefore, when Paul concludes his instructions on marriage, that he states, "This is a profound mystery—but I am talking about Christ and the church"?

Throughout the Bible, God uses many different kinds of images to help us understand the various aspects of our relationship with Him. He describes himself as our Father, our Shepherd, our Master and Lord, our Servant, our Brother, etc. It is always God's relationship to man. Here, and only here, He uses the image of Christ and the Church to illustrate His relationship to the church, His bride. The Christian marriage is intended by God to be a daily, living illustration of the love Christ has for the church. We can only do this by committing to love sacrificially, purely, carefully, and tenderly.

Early in my Christian life, I was always busily engaged in serving the Lord. I was constantly concerned about the kind of witness I was being for the Lord. Unfortunately, it never occurred to me that I needed to have that same concern for my witness as a Christian husband. Did other people see Jesus in me by the way I treated my wife? It was only after I began to do an in-depth study through the epistle of 1 Timothy that I began to see its importance. As I studied Paul's detailed requirements for those who were qualified to serve as leaders in the church, I began to understand the importance of a God-glorifying family life:

> Now the overseer must be above reproach, the husband of but one wife. . . . He must manage his own family well and see that his children obey him with proper respect. (If anyone does not know how to manage his own family, how can he take care of God's church?) (1 Timothy 3:2,4,5).

I was suddenly challenged, "Do I know how to 'manage' my family, God's way?"

What does it mean to "manage" one's family? In the Greek, the word is *proistemi*. It means "to be over, to superintend, preside over; to be a protector or guardian; to give aid; to care for, give attention to." I had the "be over, superintend, preside over" part down pretty well. It was the other areas of "protecting, guarding, aiding, caring for, giving attention to" that I was lacking. Essentially, I was too self-centered in my attitude toward my family to enable God to be glorified or for my marriage to be blessed. No wonder my wife didn't honor me the way I thought she should. God wasn't moving her to honor me because I wasn't honoring Him. The Bible teaches us to "Give everyone what you owe him: . . . if respect, then respect; if honor, then honor" (Romans 13:7). In my case, my wife was losing respect for me until I began to strive to apply Christlike love to my family. The change wasn't instantaneous. It didn't come because I declared to my wife that I was a changed man. It happened little by little, as I gave God permission to confront error in my life. I had to allow Him to teach me a new way of relating to my wife and children. It was no longer okay for me to love sacrificially and unconditionally those outside my home and be selfish and inwardly focused when I was alone with my family. As I focused upon being a husband and father who glorified God, my family slowly began to honor and respect me. This is where our next chapter will lead us.

7

Wives Of
Unmatched Beauty

However, each of you also must love his wife as he loves himself, and the wife must respect her husband. Wives, in the same way be submissive to your husbands so that, if any of them do not believe the word, they may be won over without words by the behavior of their wives, when they see the purity and reverence of your lives. Your beauty should not come from outward adornment, such as braided hair and the wearing of gold jewelry and fine clothes. Instead, it should be that of your inner self, the unfading beauty of a gentle and quiet spirit, which is of great worth in God's sight. For this is the way the holy women of the past who put their hope in God used to make themselves beautiful. They were submissive to their own husbands, like Sarah, who obeyed Abraham and called him her master. You are her daughters if you do what is right and do not give way to fear (1 Peter 3:1-6).

The late female comedian, Sophie Tucker, once outlined what a woman needed to be respected by men: From age 0 to 18 years, she needs good parents; from 18 to 35 years, she needs good looks; from 35 to 55 years, she needs a good personality; from 55 on she needs lots of cash. In this comical way, she summarized what becomes the driving obsession of most women within our culture: The need to be loved, accepted and respected by men. Yet, in our culture, obsessed with outward appearances, this becomes a glass mountain. If women are able to scale the peak (and few are), they know sooner or later they will slip from its apex to the valley below. This is true even for the most physically beautiful women. Unmatched beauty is unattainable for most because of genetics; and for the few who inherit it, it never lasts. Age, gravity and the ever-changing definitions of what "beautiful" is make it a phantom for most women.

If you ask the average woman if she is beautiful, she will tell you, "No." Maybe that is the reason the pursuit of physical beauty becomes so intense. American women spend over 20 billion dollars a year on cosmetics and another 30 billion on diets. Add to that the number of plastic surgeries, liposuctions and implants, and the pursuit of beauty easily becomes one of our major industries.

Long ago, wise and godly men and women came to recognize the folly of such pursuits. It was Solomon, surrounded by beautiful women, who wrote, "Favor is deceitful, and beauty is vain: but a woman that feareth the LORD, she shall be praised" (Proverbs 31:30, KJV).

The focus of Peter's teachings on marriage is upon beauty—the beauty that never ages or fades, rather, it tends to become more attractive with time. He calls it "unfading beauty of a gentle and quiet spirit, which is of great worth in God's sight."

In an earlier chapter, I went into great detail explaining the unique differences that exist between men and women. There are also some things which men and women have in common. One of them is the need to be respected, especially by their spouses.

The universal fear of every woman is that she will become an object—to be used and abused—rather than being valued and cared for as a person of worth. Conversely, every man fears being subjugated and dominated by a female. We might call this the universal male neurosis. Every man has a fear of falling short of the expectations of his beloved—being weighed in the balance and found wanting—in some or all of his roles.

Because of this difference in perspective, men and women seek respect in very different ways. For women, respect is experienced though gentleness, affection, caring, thoughtfulness and tenderness. For men, it comes through acceptance, esteem and approval. It is because of these differences that Peter had very different instructions to give to men and women in 1 Peter 3:1-7. He begins by speaking to the wives. They are exhorted to show respect through their actions, their attitudes and their appearances.

How wives show respect to their husbands

When one sets out to interpret a Bible passage, it is important to begin by establishing the context in which it was given. Peter begins the third chapter of his first letter by stating, "Wives, in the same way be submissive to your husbands." What does he mean when he says "in the same way"? He is referring back to the instructions that he had given previously; Peter had outlined what it means to follow in Jesus' steps. It involves being Holy (1:13-16), being Loving (1:22), being Forgiving (2:1), being Pure (2:11,12), being Submissive to Authority (2:13), being God's Servant (2:16). He concluded in verses 2:21-23 by exhorting:

> To this you were called, because Christ suffered for you, leaving you an example, that you should follow in his steps. He committed no sin, and no deceit was found in his mouth. When they hurled their insults at Him, He did not retaliate; when He suffered, He made no threats. Instead, He entrusted Himself to Him who judges justly (1 Peter 2:21-23).

Why was this so critical for these wives? Because in their particular situation, they were married to men who "do not believe the word . . . ." These were men who did not have a personal relationship with Jesus Christ and had no respect for the Bible and its teachings. Peter identifies the primary object for these wives to lead their husbands to faith in Christ and to do it "without words by the behavior of their wives."

Ladies, it is important to note that God's purpose for you, according to Peter, is not to first make the man a better husband. Rather, it is to win him to Christ. We can assume that, if Christ really gets a hold of a man's life, in time he will become a better husband, because he will become a better Christian. But the woman's first concern should be her husband's relationship with Christ, not with her.

Loving actions

How is she to accomplish this task? By her actions! The Living Bible expresses it this way: "Your godly lives will speak to them better than any words." Most women are far more verbal than men. They are more accustomed to expressing their feelings verbally. As a result, women can often pummel men with words in an effort to express their thoughts and feelings. Many men have become intimidated by their wive's faith and zeal for God. Peter counsels wives to follow a different, more effective tactic; let him see it in your actions toward him.

The Amplified translation helps us to identify more specifically what actions he is speaking of:

> When they observe the pure and modest way in which you conduct yourselves, together with your reverence [for your husband. That is, you are to feel for him all that reverence includes]—to respect, defer to, revere him; [revere means] to honor, esteem (appreciate, prize), and [in the human sense] adore him; [and adore means] to admire, praise, be devoted to, deeply love and enjoy [your husband].

I don't know a man in the world who wouldn't be affected by a woman who treated him in the way described above.

I know many of you would call this "Mission Impossible." You, frankly, may be so embittered toward your husband that the thought of "admiring" him or "enjoying" him as stated above is completely out of the question. But remember what Paul said in Ephesians 5:21, "Submit to one another out of reverence for Christ." Such a loving and respectful attitude toward your husband needs to find its primary motivation from a desire to honor and serve God through Christ Jesus—just as John said, "We love because He first loved us" (1 John 4:19). So also wives need to begin by first loving God and then loving their husbands for Christ's sake.

Some women have told me that they feel like hypocrites, pretending to feel things for their husbands that they don't feel. They feel they are being dishonest. It would be dishonest and dishonorable if you were motivated by selfish reasons to manipulate or deceive, but this is not the case here. The Spirit-filled woman is seeking to manifest Christ in her relationships with all, including and especially her husband. It is allowing Christ to love your husband through you.

It is important to understand that we should not be controlled by our feelings. Feelings are not the source but the result of our beliefs and actions. If you believe that someone loves you, you will feel good about them and act lovingly toward them. If you think someone hates you, you will feel threatened and hurt and behave cautiously and guardedly around them.

Likewise, if you believe that God loves you and He is watching out for you and will protect you, it becomes safe to obey Him. His commands to love and respect others (including your spouse) become safe. You love out of necessity, because you desire to please Him. Your spouse becomes the object of your love, not the reason or cause for loving. We love because Christ first loved us (1 John 4:19), not because someone has become lovable. In a sense, we begin to love others as a vicarious expression of our love for Christ.

Ironically, when we begin to act in a loving manner toward someone, loving "feelings" soon begin to develop. We start seeing them with different eyes. Likewise, they begin, sometimes very slowly, to respond to being loved.

This may take some people a very long time because they have never learned how to freely love another person. But it works, especially in marriage. Why? Let me illustrate. All men yearn to be loved and esteemed by their wives. In many ways, men are still little boys, looking for maternal approval. We desperately need the love and acceptance of our wives. Sometimes the behavior men display seems to say just the opposite. Our defensiveness, impatience or irritability reads to a woman like rejection or disfavor. In most cases, it is the result of our own fears of not measuring up to our wive's expectations for us as husbands and fathers. This is why men do not respond well to criticism and fault-finding! The caricature of the nagging wife is the bane of husbandhood. She is the symbol of our inadequacy as men. Conversely, when a woman shows (especially publicly) her love and devotion for her husband, his sense of worth soars.

Pure and reverent attitude

Peter follows his exhortation to Christlike action by addressing the attitude which should control a wife's thoughts. He speaks of "when they see the purity and reverence of your lives." How does one go about living a "pure and reverent" life? It requires more than just doing it. It begins with the right attitude!

What do I mean by "attitude"? We often speak of "attitude" to explain the way a person outwardly manifests his/her personality, usually negatively. I often hear my grown children talk about someone having an "attitude." Technically speaking, we all have an attitude, because attitude is more than just what we reveal outwardly. It begins with what we believe inwardly to be the truth. Whatever we believe to be the truth about a person or thing will determine our viewpoint, our perspective of them, which in turn dictates our thoughts, our feelings and our actions. That is why we teach that Christ changes lives from the inside, out. As a person comes to believe in God through Christ, as he begins to trust in the truth and reliability of God's Word, the Bible, he begins to behave differently. That's because our basic nature is to emulate what we believe to be the best way, the way of truth.

One of the great dangers spiritually is to believe something is true when in fact it is false. Jesus warned, "But if your eyes are bad, your whole body will be full of darkness. If then the light within you is darkness, how great is that darkness!" (Matthew 6:23). One of life's tragic errors is to base your choices in life upon falsehoods rather than upon the firm truth of God's Word. Jesus likened it to building your house upon the sandy soil of the beach rather than on the rock cliffs above. When life's storms come, and they always do, they will quickly destroy the life built upon the shifting foundations of the fads and fashions of this present world. This is why it is so important to base our marriages upon the sure foundation of God's Word, rather than on what Paul called "the fashion of this world."

In today's world, it is "fashionable" to cut and run when a marriage begins to face difficulties. We use phrases like "irreconcilable differences," or "incompatibility." We tell ourselves and others that "the love is gone" and then excuse ourselves from trying any more. In contrast, God offers a totally different prescription to women who are facing such conflicts. He says, begin developing a "pure and reverent" attitude. This begins when you start loving God with all your heart and when you focus upon being a reflection of who He is in all your relationships and not upon the sins and failings of others. Then we begin to see the lovelessness of others as a challenge of discipleship, as one endeavors to fulfill Jesus' command, "If anyone would come after me, he must deny himself and take up his cross and follow me" (Matthew 16:24).

If I am going to have a pure and reverent attitude, I must begin by believing right things which will produce that kind of attitude. Where does that begin? By believing that God's Word on marriage is not archaic and male-centered but rather the infallible truth of God; and secondly, that pleasing God is the most profitable, personally beneficial thing I can do. As the author of Hebrews says, "without faith it is impossible to please God, because anyone who comes to Him must believe that He exists and that He rewards those who earnestly seek Him" (Hebrews 11:6). A life of purity and reverence by itself will never hold any real attraction. To live pure and reverent lives means swimming against the current of our world. It requires self-control, denial and sacrifice. We all know that such a life does not come easily, for they are the works of a "crucified life"! Yet, if I believe that godliness is "great reward" (greater reward than self-indulgence, self-seeking, or any other kind of "self" motive) then purity and reverence will percolate naturally to the surface of my life.

One of the challenges women face in living purely and reverently before God is their natural desire to please their husbands. I Corinthians 7:34 states:

> An unmarried woman or virgin is concerned about the Lord's affairs: Her aim is to be devoted to the Lord in both body and spirit. But a married woman is concerned about the affairs of this world—how she can please her husband.

It is not a sin for her to want to please her husband, but many women have compromised their faith and spiritual commitments in an effort to avoid conflict with their husbands. I have seen this happen in two different ways. One, she may neglect personal Bible study and prayer and other essential parts of her daily Christian life if her husband objects. Or secondly, she may agree to behave or participate in things that are contrary to her beliefs, out of a desire to please or satisfy her husband's desires. This only causes the man to lose respect for his wife and will leave her in a condition of sin, because "everything that does not come from faith is sin" (Romans 14:23).

God wants us to display a maturity in our understanding. That means women need to direct in a healthy and godly manner the desire to please their husbands. It becomes essential that a woman maintain her personal spiritual disciplines so she can grow and become a God-centered and controlled woman. Only then will she be able to manifest the "fragrance of Christ" in her actions and attitude. Remember, the primary objective is not to make her husband love her but to bring him to love Christ. If he falls in love with Christ, he will love her also, with the unconditional love of the Spirit.

By now, we all should recognize that the love of the flesh is shallow, selfish and short-lived. Look instead for that which transcends the flesh—the lasting love of the Spirit of God.

An appearance of inner beauty

Last of all, Peter addresses the issue of outward appearance. At various times, this has been a very controversial issue because Christians have had difficulty coming to agreement over what is the appropriate appearance and apparel for the Christian woman. Billy Graham probably provided the clearest commentary when he responded to this issue by saying, "I believe a woman should dress as the world dresses, but not undress as the world undresses." That comment alone probably freed millions of Christian women to dress in a contemporary and attractive manner without unnecessary guilt. It is also in close agreement with what Peter was saying.

Peter was not condemning women for being beautiful or for looking as attractive as possible. I have known Christian women who, in their desire to display holiness, neglected their appearance or purposely hid their attractiveness. The unfortunate side effect was that it made them far more an object of curious interest than a testimony to holiness.

Rather, Peter instructs, "Your beauty should not come from outward adornment . . . . Instead, it should be that of your inner self, the unfading beauty of a gentle and quiet spirit, which is of great worth in God's sight" (1 Peter 3:3,4).

As Greek scholar Kenneth Wuest explained in his Word Studies in the Greek, "What the Word of God forbids the Christian woman is a conspicuous, extravagant, intricate artificiality in the manner of wearing the hair . . . covering their person with a lavish and conspicuous display of jewelry . . . and the donning of . . . clothing that the world wore, immodest, gaudy, conspicuous."[16] Note how he repeatedly used the word "conspicuous" to describe the kind of adornment women were not to wear. The word refers to anything that draws attention to itself. The object of a godly man or woman should never be to draw attention to themselves through any means. There is nothing wrong with wearing an attractive and contemporary hair style or clothing or jewelry. But if it becomes gaudy, showy or conspicuous, as a means to either draw attention to ourselves or to mask the shallowness of our character, we are in error. Our desire should be to draw attention to Christ in us and not to our bodies or person.

When a woman relies upon her outward appearance to catch and keep her man, she is leaning her ladder against the wrong wall. First of all, none of us can retain our youth and beauty forever. Because of the aging process and gravity, sooner or later, the sags, dips and bulges win out over us all. Secondly, outward beauty can only hold a man's interest for a short time. Believe it or not, ladies, the average man IS interested in more than just your body. In fact, he is not nearly as concerned about your dress size as you are.

Some time ago, I was listening to a radio program, and the host was reading the results of a survey that had come in over the AP line. In this survey, a large number of men were asked, "What is the most attractive part of a woman's body?" There didn't seem to be a clear consensus among men on this question. Each had his preference. But it was the second question they asked that really surprised me: "What is the most important factor in your choice of a woman?" Can you guess what the answer was? The vast majority of men stated, "Personality."

Please believe me, ladies, I speak as a man who knows men well. Men are far more attracted to who you are as a person than your outward appearance. I would be lying to say that men don't notice outward appearance, but it can't hold their attention or their hearts. Men are far more visual than women are. They can get very excited over something they see, but that does not mean they are committed to something just because it has caught their eye. When it comes to lasting relationships, "parts is parts"! Men love the women they like. Companionship and fellowship is far more important than body type.

Therefore, it makes all the sense in the world not to make your outward appearance your primary source of identity and worth. Rather, let it be "your inner self, the unfading beauty of a gentle and quiet spirit," that you are most concerned about.

Such is not only of great worth before God, but it is also what is most important to your husband. Again, this doesn't mean you should neglect or ignore your outward appearance, but when a woman adorns her outward person with regard to honoring God, there is a beautiful consistency between her inward attitude and her outward testimony.

Along this same line, Kenneth Wuest adds, "Personality is after all far more important than either physical beauty or the adornment which mere clothing affords. A person ought to be bigger than any consideration of outward decoration. One can dress up a fence post. If one finds it necessary to depend upon either physical beauty or clothing in order to make a favorable impression upon others, that fact shows that that person realizes his lack of those personal and spiritual qualities that make a virile Christian character."[17]

At this point, Peter turns to an ancient illustration to inspire his female readers. Unfortunately, our lack of understanding of his comments has had, for some, the opposite effect. It is actually a continuation of Peter's comments on adornment. It is the adornment of submission!

Submission

The teaching of wifely submission has become increasingly controversial over the last several years. It has come under attack as being oppressive and chauvinistic. I must say, this is not how the Bible presents it. In large part, the Bible views it in terms of positions or roles of responsibility. God has placed men in the leadership role within the marriage and the family. Wives are called to serve under and support that leadership role. I believe it is vitally important that men and women understand and accept these differences in roles in the family structure. Oftentimes the conflict that exists between a husband and wife stems from the lack of understanding or acceptance of this God-ordained pattern. Gene Getz, in his book *The Measure of the Family*, puts it well:

> God's theological statements, when interpreted correctly, will normally work in harmony with the psychological nature of man. When these theological and psychological laws are violated, man cannot reach his complete potential in terms of inner security and happiness . . . . He (God) has established certain roles for family members, and if we violate them we will not find true happiness. Our present frustrations and anxieties will only be accentuated and will eventually turn to bitterness and disillusionment.[18]

In light of that, let's go through the process of "correctly interpreting" what the Bible teaches regarding wifely submission.

There are two words used in the New Testament to describe this area of relationship between a husband and wife. The first is *hupotasso*. It is a Greek military term meaning "to arrange [troop divisions] in a military fashion under the command of a leader." In non-military use, it was "a voluntary attitude of giving in, cooperating, assuming responsibility, and carrying a burden." The second is *hupeiko*. It means "to resist no longer, but to give way, yield (of combatants), to yield to authority and admonition, to submit."

We find that both these words are used to describe how Christ submitted and was subject to the Father, citizens being subject to rulers and others in governmental authority, how

Christians are to be submissive and subject to one another, of employee to employers, children obeying parents, as well as wives to husbands. In each case, submission applies the responsibility to give to, love and serve others. The manner in which one fulfills this requirement differs with regard to the varying authority structures, but the attitude of placing oneself under another's authority applies equally.

What is it?

What exactly is wifely submission? It is, first of all, the recognition of the husband's God-given role and authority as the leader of the home. This requires a woman to "yield" to her husband whenever he chooses to exercise his authority. She should not seek to dominate, control or to manipulate him to satisfy her will. Submission is the opposite of being self-assertive. It means that a woman is teachable and vulnerable.

What it is not!

Conversely, there are many things which submission is NOT about. Submission does not mean that a man has the right to abuse his wife physically, emotionally, verbally, psychologically, sexually, or in any other way. It is tragic that I should have to make such a statement. Unfortunately, many abusive husbands have used the Bible's teaching on submission to justify their behavior. This is profane and blasphemous. Abuse is first of all SIN. Secondly, it is CRIMINAL. Assault is a felony offense, punishable by imprisonment. It is never, never, ever right or justified!

Submission also does not mean that a woman cannot have her own opinions or point of view. She does not have to agree with her husband on everything. She does not have to submit to anything that violates her conscience, morals or ethics, nor is she required to defend her husband when he is wrong. In fact, one of the most loving and submissive things a woman can do is to confront error in her husband when she sees that an attitude or a behavior is harmful to him and/or his family.

God's intention is for marriage to be a partnership, but for the purpose of order, he has placed the man as the final authority within the home, after God's Word, of course. A wise man will use his wife as a stabilizer in his role as leader. We will deal with the man's responsibilities further in the next chapter.

So what does Peter mean when he tells the wives "For this is the way the holy women of the past who put their hope in God used to make themselves beautiful. They were submissive to their own husband" (1 Peter 3:5)? He explains himself in the next verse by using the example of Sarah: "like Sarah, who obeyed Abraham and called him her master. You are her daughters if you do what is right and do not give way to fear" (1 Peter 3:6). To understand how submission makes a woman beautiful, we need to take a look at how the Bible deals with the contrasting natures of physical beauty and "the beauty of holiness."

Human beauty has two grave weaknesses. First, it usually produces an attitude of pride and rebellion in those who possess it. For example, we read of Absalom, the son of King David:

> In all Israel there was not a man so highly praised for his handsome appearance as Absalom. From the top of his head to the sole of his foot there was no blemish in him (2 Samuel 14:25).

He rebelled against David his father, overthrew him and attempted to establish himself as king in his place. Likewise, in Lucifer whom we see the ultimate example of pride and rebellion, we read, "You were the model of perfection, full of wisdom and perfect in beauty" (Ezekiel 28:12). So it is throughout the Bible, references are repeatedly made to those who are snared by their physical beauty.

Because of this, Solomon makes this observation: "Charm is deceptive, and beauty is fleeting; but a woman who fears the LORD is to be praised" (Proverbs 31:30). The beauty that is repeatedly praised in the Bible is "the beauty of holiness" (1 Chronicles 16:29; 2 Chronicles 20:21; Psalm 29:2). That is because the Holy God is the one who is "perfect in beauty" (Psalm 50:2). It is He who declares, "Man looks at the outward appearance, but the LORD looks at the heart" (1 Samuel 16:7).

What Peter is telling us is that these ancient women, like Sarah, became beautiful to God through their pursuit of a pure and reverent life—a life of holiness!

It is probably necessary to add that physical beauty is not the only stumbling block for people. There are also the issues of wealth and intellect. These areas as well can become false foundations upon which we seek to establish our lives and strive to find meaning and worth. They are really variant forms of human beauty. Wealth is "material beauty," and intellect is "mental beauty." In other words, we consider anyone who has great wealth (at least greater than our own) or high intellect to be of greater worth than those of lesser attainment.

Often parents and others push their children in these directions, telling them these are the pathways of happiness and fulfillment, or just necessary for being "well-adjusted." Well, they may help us adjust to this world's value system, but they are not the key to being well-adjusted with God. God wants us to be like Jesus. As far as beauty went, "He hath no form nor comeliness; and when we shall see Him, there is no beauty that we should desire Him" (Isaiah 53:2, KJV); with regard to material prosperity, "though He was rich, yet for your sakes He became poor, that ye through His poverty might be rich" (2 Corinthians 8:9, KJV); and when we consider intellect, we are told, "For our rejoicing is this, the testimony of our conscience, that in simplicity and godly sincerity, not with fleshly wisdom, but by the grace of God, we have had our conversation in the world, and more abundantly to you-ward" (2 Corinthians 1:12, KJV).

Sarah called Abraham Lord?

What throws most of today's women a curve is the phrase, "Like Sarah, who obeyed Abraham and called him her master." The Authorized Version reads even worse. It states, "Even as Sara obeyed Abraham, calling him lord" (1 Peter 3:6, KJV). The problem is easily resolved, once we realize that the Greek *kurios*, translated "lord" or "master," although used to describe the Savior, was also used to denote any person who sat in authority over others. Peter is not telling wives that they must also call their husbands "lord." Rather, Sarah used it as a wifely courtesy to her husband, as a recognition of his authority over her. Peter's focus is not upon what she said, but the submissiveness of heart from which her words came. To speak in such a way today in our culture would be inappropriate and misleading, as is evidenced by the confusion many have when they first read it.

Fear only fear!

Peter closes with these words: "You are her daughters if you do what is right and do not give way to fear" (1 Peter 3:6). It is the last part of this statement that is a little unclear, especially in the Authorized Version, which is more literal. It reads "afraid with any amazement." In the original, there are two words used to express this "fear and amazement" which these women might fall victim to: 1. *phobeo*, which means "to put to flight by terrifying (to scare away), to be struck with fear, to be seized with alarm"; and 2. *ptoesis*, to be afraid of with terror.

The emotion which Peter is identifying was translated by one reliable commentator as "fluttering terror."[19] He cross-references it with Proverbs 3:25, where we read, "Have no fear of sudden disaster or of the ruin that overtakes the wicked" (Proverbs 3:25).

Alford suggests the following interpretation: "As long as the believing wives are doing good, they need not be afraid with any sudden terror on the account which their unbelieving husbands may exact from them."[20] This fits well with the Amplified's offering: "not giving way to hysterical fears or letting anxieties unnerve you."

It seems that Peter's words are a warning not to yield to fear in face of the challenge facing these wives. It was President Franklin Roosevelt who once sought to calm a frightened nation by saying, "We have nothing to fear but fear itself." Why is fear such a threat? Because it elicits a panic response, provoking us to flee when we should stand and resist. Peter is encouraging wives not to give in to their fears, whether they are spawned by threat or discouragement. As Paul exhorted the Corinthians, "Therefore, my dear brothers, stand firm. Let nothing move you. Always give yourselves fully to the work of the Lord, because you know that your labor in the Lord is not in vain" (1 Corinthians 15:58). The promise of both Paul and Peter is that God will reward the woman who stands fast in her convictions to live as a woman of God, regardless of the disposition of her husband. To that, I should add Paul's words to Timothy, "For God did not give us a spirit of timidity, but a spirit of power, of love and of self-discipline" (2 Timothy 1:7). It is in this power which the Bible challenges us all to stand and not the power of the flesh. The flesh will eventually give in to its fears, but the Spirit of God instills power, love and self-control!

8

Men Whom Women
Love To Love

Husbands, in the same way be considerate as
you live with your wives, and treat them with respect as the
weaker partner and as heirs with you of the gracious gift of
life, so that nothing will hinder your prayers (1 Peter 3:7).

In the New Testament, there is a principle called ethical reciprocity. It means that the Bible never puts all the responsibility in a relationship upon only one party. In every relationship there are mutual obligations.

Ethical refers to "behavior that is morally right." Ethics is morality applied to our daily lives. We behave ethically when we choose to do the right thing, to behave in a morally consistent manner.

A principle is a comprehensive and fundamental rule. Gravity is a principle. Whether you believe in it or not, it is still there, still true, still in effect. Try to defy it by jumping off a high building without proper equipment, and you will lose. Gravity will win every time.

An Ethical Principle is a morally correct behavior that is mandated by God. If we violate it, it will cause negative consequences. We may not even recognize the cause of many of our problems because we are ignorant of God's principles—like those of whom the prophet Hosea spoke: ". . . my people are destroyed from lack of knowledge. Because you have rejected knowledge, I also reject you . . . because you have ignored the law of your God, I also will ignore your children" (Hosea 4:6).

We see Ethical Reciprocity expressed throughout the Old and New Testaments. In every relationship, both parties are held accountable for specific obligations of behavior.

For example, when Paul speaks about the rules for holy living in Colossians 3:18-4:1 and in Ephesians 5:22-6:9, he has something to say to both sides of each social relationship.

Colossians	Ephesians

In the home:

Col. 3:18 Wives, submit to your husbands, as is fitting in the Lord.	Eph. 5:22 Wives, submit to your husbands as to the Lord.
Col. 3:19 Husbands, love your wives and do not be harsh with them.	Eph. 5:25 Husbands, love your wives, just as Christ loved the church and gave himself up for her.
Col. 3:20 Children, obey your parents in everything, for this pleases the Lord.	Eph. 6:1 Children, obey your parents in the Lord, for this is right.
Col. 3:21 Fathers, do not embitter your children, or they will become discouraged.	Eph. 6:4 Fathers, do not exasperate your children; instead, bring them up in the training and instruction of the Lord.

On the job:

Col. 3:22 Slaves, obey your earthly masters in everything; and do it, not only when their eye is on you and to win their favor, but with sincerity of heart and reverence for the Lord.	Eph. 6:5 Slaves, obey your earthly masters with respect and fear, and with sincerity of heart, just as you would obey Christ.

Col. 4:1 Masters, provide your
slaves with what is right and
fair, because you know that you
also have a Master in heaven.

Eph. 6:9 And masters, treat
your slaves in the same way.

Obligation of love

In the previous chapter, we talked at great length about the responsibility of wives toward their husbands. It naturally follows that Peter would conclude with a summary of the obligations of husbands toward their wives.

It should be obvious to us why Peter has done this. The natural tendency of our selfish natures is to focus upon others' obligations toward us and to overlook our obligations toward them.

At times, it is comical to watch husbands and wives as they sit together during a marriage seminar. When I focus upon the man's responsibilities, I can see the eyes of women glancing up at their husbands. In some cases, elbow jabs into the ribs of a husband become visible, rocking some poor fellow in his seat. It's his wife's way of saying, "Are you listening to what he is saying? It's what I have been telling you for years."

As soon as the topic shifts to the women, the guys begin to make knowing faces. They smile condescendingly toward their wives. It's now their turn to say, "See? What have I been telling you all along? See, I was right! It's all your fault!"

But when we look at the balance the Bible presents, we find that both are right, and both are wrong. Each has his or her role to play and obligations to fulfill.

In the broadest sense, they each have an obligation to love one another. Paul commands: "Let no debt remain outstanding, except the continuing debt to love one another, for he who loves his fellow-man has fulfilled the law" (Romans 13:8).

Loving one another is not an option. It is an obligation that must be paid, just like your house or car payment. In this case, the one who is demanding payment is God. If you neglect or refuse to make payment, He will hold you accountable.

Over time, if you neglect your obligation long enough, you will begin to accrue a huge emotional/relational debt. You will become like a man running from his creditors. You will avoid people and situations that confront you with your lovelessness. You may change where you sit in church or the place you enter and leave by. You may decide to change churches altogether. You may stop socializing together or carpooling together, all because you don't want to face the obligation of loving someone who has sinned against you or whom you have sinned against.

The Bible describes this condition as a "root of bitterness." Listen to what the author of Hebrews says about it: "See to it that no one misses the grace of God and that no bitter root grows up to cause trouble and defile many" (Hebrews 12:15). He is describing the end results of a heart given over to bitterness. It is essentially emotional bankruptcy! To be bitter is to forsake God's grace, and as a consequence to become "troubled" and "defiled." At first you become estranged from the person. Eventually, you become estranged from God. It doesn't happen quickly, rather it is a slow, erosive thing, a subtle deterioration, a tragic degeneration.

Because it happens almost imperceptibly, it is critically important to address "bitterness" as soon as we see its buds of lovelessness manifest toward others. Left unchecked, it will spread and "defile" your whole being. (The Greek word for "defile" [miaino] means "to dye with another color, to stain, to defile, pollute, sully, contaminate, soil." It pictures the white robes of righteousness becoming marred by a stain). Can you picture in your mind a beautiful young bride walking down the aisle at her wedding, then you notice there is a great big black grease spot in the middle of her dress. Everyone's attention would be immediately drawn to this mark. The beauty of the moment, its splendor and majesty, would be lost because of such a terrible distraction.

Bitterness is a terrible distraction and detraction to our lives in Christ (not to mention our marriages). Confess it, for bitterness destroys marriages.

Leadership crisis

In the sci-fi movies of the 1950s, the Martian invader was expected to approach the Earthling and give the command, "Take me to your leader!" Apparently, the Martian could not tell one Earthling from another. He had no idea what the distinguishing characteristics of a leader were.

That pretty much describes the dilemma most men face today as they attempt to figure out what it means to be the leaders of their homes. In the past, they might confidently look at the kind of husband their father was. Not any more! Today, such fathers are viewed as a relic of the past. Add to that our distrust of national leaders and institutions (we tend to expect deceit and duplicity from them), and the average man is left without role models or heroes.

Ironically, our only heroes today are anti-heroes. We used to call them the bad guys. Now bad is good; and the Bible tells us that's not good! Isaiah 5:20 warns, "Woe to those who call evil good and good evil, who put darkness for light and light for darkness, who put bitter for sweet and sweet for bitter" (Isaiah 5:20). It sounds like a description of our topsy-turvy, turn-around, upside-down world. As one hero after another is debunked, we are left without any clear role models to follow. So where do we turn?

I hope you said, "The Bible." There, God has given to men His guidelines for becoming a man after His own heart: A man who is both the one in charge, as well as a servant and caregiver—the benevolent leader who is both guardian and shepherd over his flock.

So what are the man's obligations? First Peter 3:7 identifies four behaviors which are incumbent upon Christian husbands: consideration, co-heirs, co-partnering and prayer!

Be considerate!

Peter begins his brief but ardent exhortation to husbands by commanding them to "be considerate as you live with your wives . . . ." If you are using an older translation, it will read somewhat differently: "Likewise, ye husbands, dwell with them according to knowledge . . . ." (1 Peter 3:7, KJV).

In some ways, this rendering is fuller than the NIV, but I prefer the Amplified for the clearest expression of what Peter wants to communicate: "In the same way you married men should live considerately with [your wives], with an intelligent recognition [of the marriage relation]." What interests me most about this translation is how it combines being considerate and intelligent. It's as if Peter is saying, "Men, the smart husbands are the ones who are considerate."

The big question is, "What exactly does it mean to be considerate?" Basically it's to be "thoughtful of others and their feelings." It infers that there is careful, well-considered, deliberate thought given to the needs of others.

Sometimes it is easier to understand a word by looking at its antonyms. In this case, the opposite of "being considerate" is to be unloving, rough, severe, or thoughtless. Unfortunately, these are the actions that characterize many men's relationships with their wives. Why? Because it is easier to be such. It comes more naturally from our sinful and selfish natures. Acknowledge that such behavior is wrong. It is the only way to begin to effect change.

There are two important aspects of being considerate of others: 1. You give thought to their needs; and 2. You think carefully and deliberately about them. It is a discipline, a conscious choice to care, regularly and consistently, about meeting your wife's needs. She is no longer an afterthought but a forethought.

The Apostle Paul captures the idea well when he writes in Philippians 2:3, "Do nothing out of selfish ambition or vain conceit, but in humility consider others better than yourselves". Paul is calling for a major shift in our points of view. We are no longer to see our own needs as the priority but those of others. In a word, we are to be "humble."

The word that is translated "consider," is the Greek word *hegeomai*. Basically it means "to lead," but here it means more. It is to "consider of greater value, to esteem highly." When someone is a leader, or in a position of high authority, we esteem them worthy of extraordinary consideration.

The President of the United States is a good example. Look at all the effort expended to protect, provide, and care for his every need. Look at the respect shown to him. Paul uses this word to illustrate the care, consideration, concern, and respect that we are called to focus upon others. To literally view them as "better than yourself."

The battle over ambition

In order to be considerate of others, we must be willing to lay aside "selfish-ambition" and "vain conceit." This is the really tough part. Most men live for their ambitions. There are certain goals and objectives they have set their sights on and have dedicated their lives to reaching them. We often comfort ourselves over the neglect of our wives and children by promising to give them more attention once other things are further along.

It's a lot like being a passenger on an airplane. We often call this flying, but it's not. The pilots do the flying. The experience of throttling back the engines at liftoff, holding the controls, landing, changing course, navigating, etc., is never ours. We just sit there, reading, eating, watching the movie, listening to the music, talking to one another. Few of us will ever know what it's like to really fly a plane. We're only passengers, at best, spectators. Our lives revolve around going from one destination to another, but we're not actively involved in getting there.

Someone once said, "Life is in the living." For many of us, life is what passes by while we sit around waiting for it to begin. We are always saying to ourselves, "When I finish this project, goal, objective . . . then I'll have time for the other stuff." Guess what? It doesn't work that way. The opportunity to be a loving husband is here right now, today, this minute. There is no guarantee that it will be there tomorrow. Every day you neglect that responsibility, the hole gets deeper. When you finally come to your senses, the hole may be too deep to dig out of.

Make a decision this very moment to begin strategizing how to be a better husband, a better father. Believe me, the time goes by too quickly. As a father of three grown children, I speak from experience. How I wish I could go back and do it differently. I was always too busy to focus on being a good husband and father. I spent too much time out of town or at the church.

I was available for everyone else first. My wife and kids got the leftovers. God was merciful. My kids have turned out all right, but I am the one who missed out.

I have one child left at home. Early on, I decided I wouldn't make the same mistake again. As I have invested myself in the youngest one's life, I have found wonderful fulfillment and joy as a parent that I largely missed with my other children. But the experience is double-edged. It also serves as a frequent reminder of what I could have had with my other children if I hadn't been so full of "vain conceit."

That's what the problem is, you know. I was so full of myself; my goals were so important that I expected everyone else's needs to follow mine. I didn't really understand Jesus' words when he said, "It is more blessed to give than receive."

The world is full of "takers"; the church is full of "takers"; families are full of "takers." It's our nature. God wants givers! You can easily recognize the givers. They are the ones who are smiling. They have joy in their lives. They sleep well because they have peace in their hearts. Sure they go through difficult stretches in life's road. But they have so much to be thankful for: they have learned that God is faithful and that life is a grand adventure.

The "takers," on the other hand, are equally recognizable. They're busy; they're important. Just ask them, they'll tell you if you have time to listen to them. They also have a lot of complaints. They can tell you what's wrong with things. Pick the topic, they have an analysis.

Which camp best describes you? I learned just soon enough that it is far better to be a "giver." Givers are getters. Takers are losers.

Wouldn't you like to join the "givers"? Decide that today will be the day. Ask God to take control of your dreams, your calendar, your portfolio, and anything else that has tyrannically controlled your life. If you ask Him, He will do it. I guarantee it.

Reap what you sow

Every man I know wants his wife to respect him and to defer to his leadership in the home. But sooner or later, respect has to be earned. All of us are naturally attracted to those who take a sincere interest in our well being. We love to talk to people who are interested in what's going on in our lives, what our feelings are, our hopes, dreams, fears. If you want your wife to respect you, start showing interest in her. Listen to her, think about her needs, provide for her care and welfare, protect her, put her needs before your own. Be a good, godly example of what it is that you want her to become.

Solomon once observed, "All this I saw, as I applied my mind to everything done under the sun. There is a time when a man lords it over others to his own hurt" (Ecclesiastes 8:9). When a man rules over his home without understanding God's way of leading, it often comes back to hurt him more than anyone else.

Too often I have listened to men complain about the churlish ways of their wives. How sad it has been for them to discover that much of what they disliked in their wives is of their own creation. These women were simply responding to their husbands' clumsy and ignorant ways of "dwelling" with them. Men, we lead by example far more than by anything we say. I know, because I have seen this lived out in my own home, too literally.

My children bear an unmistakable physical resemblance to me. This is unfortunate, because overwhelming popular consensus agrees that my wife is unquestionably the more attractive half of our marriage.

"Less-than-great-looks" can be worked with and compensated for. But negative behaviors and attitudes are more difficult to manage. When I see them coming out of my kids, I have to own that they learned them from me. Granted they have many good qualities. But the ones I notice most are the the ones that are most familiar to me, my character flaws. I didn't have to teach them these bad habits. They picked them up by hanging around me. Gentlemen (and ladies), we reap what we sow.

Be respectful

As Peter continues his inspired commentary on marriage, he cites three ways in which a man can show consideration toward his wife. The first is to treat her with respect. The second is to treat her as a co-heir in Christ. The third is to pray with her and for her.

Treat them with respect as the weaker partner (1 Peter. 3:7).

The motivation for doing this should be obvious by now. If you want respect (and every man does), then you must show it. We reap what we sow!

There are some people who are easy to respect. They behave in such a way as to deserve it. Then there are those to whom we show respect only because of their position. It is preferable in a marriage that a man show respect to his wife because she deserves it, and in the vast majority of marriages, this is the case. But there are some where the wife is not behaving in a way that is honorable—you still owe her the respect due her as your wife.

I know there are some who are reading this and thinking, "How can I show respect when I don't feel it inside?" Well, you can always fake it! No, I don't really mean that, exactly. What I do mean is that we cannot allow our behavior to become enslaved to our feelings. There are many things we do because they are the right thing to do, not because it's what we feel like doing. Showing respect to our wives needs to be one of those things.

If you have a habit of focusing on your wife's weaknesses and faults, this is going to be a great challenge. You are going to have to ask God to give you a different set of eyes when it comes to the way you look at her. It is essential that you not wait for her to change first before you begin showing her respect. Right feelings follow right actions. As you treat her with respect, God will enable you to see reasons why this is the right direction for you to go in your relationship.

Male vs. female

Many times when my wife and I get together with friends, we will start to make jokes about the opposite sex. The women will start commenting on how weird men are; the men will cite evidence on how strange female behavior is.

Usually it is humorous and harmless. For example, my wife and daughter sometimes will poke fun at me and my sons because we are absentminded. I may go to the store on an errand and forget to pick up the primary item for which I was sent. I don't do it on purpose, it just slips my mind. There have been times when I have had to call home and ask my wife what it was I was supposed to pick up. It's a bit embarrassing, but it's far better than coming home empty-handed.

Not infrequently, I will get the wrong brand or size of product. If my wife doesn't specify the exact size, brand and contents, chances are better than not that I will pick up the wrong thing. My wife and daughter will laugh and say, "It must be a guy thing."

To a degree, this is due to inherent differences between men and women, but it is also due to the fact that my wife and I are very different people. My wife is a detail person, and I am learning. It comes naturally to her; I have to work at it. I hate to admit it, but we spent years criticizing and disrespecting one another because of our differences in this and other areas. She could not understand what was so difficult in picking up an 8-ounce can of stewed tomatoes. Why had I returned home with a 10-ounce can of tomato sauce? To me, anything that said "tomato" worked.

Over time, I have come to realize that my wife's attention to details has kept our ship afloat more times than I would like to admit. For her part, she has made great efforts to "help my infirmity." She writes lists and instructional notes. She puts "post-it notes" in places where they can't be missed. She has learned to remind me as I am going out the door, even at times making me "repeat" what I am going after. This used to really "bug" me, until I finally admitted I need her help in this area.

More importantly, I have come to recognize the wisdom of God in bringing us together. She provides an invaluable support to me in areas where I have needed it the most. I have learned more about organization from her than any other person I know. God and my mother know how badly I needed to learn how to get organized.

Conversely, my wife has come to see value in my absent-mindedness. I am an abstract thinker. As a result, I have come up with some useful insights over the years that have helped us chart our course in life and work through some difficult situations. Some of my best sermon ideas have come during my times of mental wandering.

Unfortunately, we can develop an opinionated view of the opposite sex, causing us to be intolerant and overly critical. In my case, my forgetfulness is the result of a wandering mind. I often forget exactly what it is I am looking for. My mind drifts off into thinking about any number of things which are more important to me when fetching some non-essential from the store. When I returned home without the item for which I was sent, my wife would get angry. I couldn't understand what the big deal was.

Eventually I came to understand that my forgetfulness was interpreted by my wife as a sign that I wasn't concerned about her and her needs. I had minimized the importance of the errand because it wasn't important to me. I wasn't viewing it from her point of view. To her it was a critical item necessary to complete a task. To me it was just a can of whatever. No big deal!

As I began to evaluate my behavior, I realized what I was doing. I considered my thoughts to be of greater importance than her needs. I wasn't giving the same kind of care and attention to the things that were important to her, simply because they weren't important to me. If my forgetfulness caused her extra difficulty, I expected her to "be understanding" and not to "make such a big deal about it." But whenever the shoe was on the other foot, and she would forget something I needed or brought home the wrong item, I would get irritated.

Opposites attract

Every wife and husband brings individual strengths and weaknesses into a marriage. The great irony is that's what attracts us to one another. Their strengths are usually in areas where we are weak. Before marriage, we tend to only focus upon our beloved's strengths. On the one hand, we gloss over their weaknesses, underestimating how irritating and frustrating their weaknesses will become to us. On the other hand, we fully expect that their strength will compensate for our area of weakness. It never occurs to us that they will become irritated with our weakness in that area of our personality.

After we marry, the weaknesses begin to grow in significance. Over time, they can become so large they obscure whatever strengths we once saw in our partner. Eventually all we can see is weakness. We can't imagine what it was that we ever saw in this person. We say things like, "How could I have been so blind?" Often we conclude that they deliberately deceived us, hiding their flaws from us until they had entrapped us.

Let me point out that when you get to this point, you have probably lost perspective. Rarely are people as good, or bad, as we believe them to be. Just as every coin has two sides, so also every person has two sides—strengths and weaknesses.

The Bible anticipates this conflict and advises us: "We who are strong ought to bear with the failings of the weak and not to please ourselves" (Romans 15:1).

In writing to the Galatians, Paul counseled them how they were to confront this kind of problem and to get along with one another:

> Brothers, if someone is caught in a sin, you who are spiritual should restore him gently. But watch yourself, or you also may be tempted. Carry each other's burdens, and in this way you will fulfill the law of Christ. If anyone thinks he is something when he is nothing, he deceives himself. Each one should test his own actions. Then he can take pride in himself, without comparing himself to somebody else (Galatians 6:1-4).

Note that he doesn't say anything about trying to change the other person. Rather we are to work on changing how we react to the weaknesses that we necessarily have to deal with every day of our lives, both in marriage and other relationships.

A large part of learning to deal with one another's weaknesses is gaining insight into why they frustrate us so much. Before marriage, we often expect that our spouse is going to satisfy our every need. They will cover up my short-comings. It doesn't take long for us to realize that it doesn't work that way. They are the first to become irritated at our weaknesses. Instead of covering them up, they start demanding that we change, and fast.

Let me illustrate what I mean from my own marriage. I tend to be a very gregarious and somewhat impulsive personality. I love spontaneity and struggle with predictability. As a result, I tend to be pretty creative. I also struggle with follow-through and consistency. If a task becomes boring, it's easy for me to drop it and move on to something more interesting.

When I met my wife, she was the most steady and stable person I knew. For her, everything has a place and she has a place for everything. She will do the same things, in the same way, every day.

I saw her as ballast in my hull. She would bring steadiness into my life. Conversely, she saw in me a freedom of expression that she did not have. Here was a perfect match. I would be the guy up-front, doing all the talking and entertaining. She would manage the details behind the scene.

In many ways, this is how our relationship has worked out. But there were several unforeseen obstacles that had to be circumnavigated. Let me illustrate with a couple of examples.

One of our most common conflicts comes when we drive in the car. I love the adventure of driving fast and never taking the same route twice. I need the variety. On the other hand, she constantly reminds me of the "legal" speed limit. I respond with something about the "flow of traffic." She reminds me of how many speeding tickets I have gotten. (Of course, she has never had one.) She tells me the shortest route. I would rather "feel" my way to our destination. I know that my driving often drives my wife nuts.

A second area of common conflict has to deal with people. I love to socialize and interact with people. She loves people, but they drain her. As a consequence, I see our home as a place to entertain; she sees our home as a place to recluse. I love activity. She loves quiet. I want to watch football with guys, eating nachos and drinking diet Coke. She enjoys jigsaw puzzles next to the fireplace.

Is one way right and the other wrong? Not necessarily. In our case, we are just "wired" differently. Those differences have often provided strengths that have sustained us in times of great trial and difficulty.

They have also challenged us to face the areas of weakness in ourselves that needed to be corrected. One of my favorite passages from the book of Proverbs expresses it well: "As iron sharpens iron, so one man sharpens another" (Proverbs 27:17).

I have found that when I sharpen a tool on my grinding stone it produces a great deal of friction. The same is true when God seeks to "sharpen" an area of our life. He usually uses another person to act as the "grinder." Sparks begin to fly, the blade gets hot. But it's the only way it can be sharpened.

That's the way it is with people, too. The best changes come through the friction we experience in attempting to get close enough to truly love one another. The friction is painful. It is the desire to get relief from the pain that motivates us to make changes.

Today, I am a safer, more controlled driver. I am far less impulsive. I am very organized, and I have learned to stick to a task until it is done. I thank God for the changes in my life. But I recognize that He used my wife to make me aware of my weaknesses and to motivate me to change.

My wife is more relaxed and spontaneous. She has learned to go with the flow and to trust that my zany way of doing things often works out. We are both better people because of the conflict.

Some suggestions

I don't care how much you love someone, there are traits in their personality that will drive you crazy. It's unavoidable. The only control you have over it is how you choose to deal with it. I suggest you begin by first focusing on your partner's strengths. What does he/she bring into your marriage you aren't good at? Write it down. Make a list. Begin to thank God for the gift that this person is to your life. When you can begin to sincerely express to God your appreciation for who your spouse is, then you are ready to share it with him/her.

In time, as you consider his/her weaknesses, ask the Lord to show you ways to help him/her grow in these areas. Recognize that the things you have the most difficulty tolerating are those areas which come most easily to you. Just because they come easily to you in no way means they come easily to your spouse. Don't expect that he/she will ever be as strong or competent in those things as you are. Rather, allow your strength in that area to cover your partner's weakness. Apply 1 Peter 4:8: "Above all, love each other deeply, because love covers over a multitude of sins." In God's eyes there is something greater than being right. Its being "loving."

Weaker?

The first reason Peter gave for treating a wife with respect is because she is the weaker partner. In some ways, women are stronger than men. The first time I observed labor and delivery with my wife, it became abundantly evident to me that she had just endured something that would have killed me. If it had been me, I would have told the doctor to give me gas and wake me when it was over.

There are also other ways in which my wife is stronger than I am. She is far better at organizing data. She has far more self-control and self-discipline than I do. So what did Peter mean when he says that women are weaker?

The most obvious explanation is physical strength. Women were designed by God for distance and endurance. Men were designed for speed and strength.

It is a scientific fact that men on average develop 50 percent greater brute strength than women. I know there are some women who are stronger than some men; but men have always, and will always, dominate those areas which require greater brute strength to succeed, such as professional athletics. Men can run faster, jump higher, and lift larger loads than women.

On the other hand, women have greater endurance. Women are much better suited for walking and running long distances than men. Because they carry larger fat deposits than men (no insult intended, ladies), they have more energy reserves, enabling them to last for longer periods of time and go longer distances.

In some ways, women are also stronger emotionally than men. Men are generally better at dealing with sudden high stress. They are more effective at crisis management and emergency response than women. The Israeli Army found that in times of war, the men were far better at adapting to the mental stress of combat than were women. Men are more adept at making quick, decisive decisions in times of intense conflict.

Yet women are far better at dealing with the stress that comes from maintenance. They are less stressed by routine and monotonous tasks than are men. Women are better maintenance managers than men. While men are focusing upon the "bigger and better," women are concerned with keeping what they have running smoothly.

The distinction that Peter made is in the area of protection. A man is called to protect his wife from anything that might threaten or endanger her. Literally, he should be committed and prepared to give his life for her. God has given him greater physical strength and capacity to respond to emergencies, so that he might protect her.

One of the ways we prepare ourselves for this role is by being gentlemanly. I believe that a man should open doors for a woman—that includes car doors. He should help her to her seat when they sit down to eat, at home and in a restaurant. Men, when we do these kinds of things, we communicate to our wives that we accept our responsibility to provide her protection, we are committed to her safety.

This is why physical abuse produces the opposite results a man desires from a relationship. Nothing will cause a woman to draw back more completely than fear of her husband. By being gentlemanly, we assure her that she is safe. She sees his embraces as a place of safety and comfort.

> ... treat them with respect ... as heirs with you of the gracious gift of life...(1 Peter 3:7).

A second reason Peter gave for treating wives with great consideration and respect is their spiritual equality within the family of God.

The Gospel revolutionized the way women were traditionally viewed. Because men possess greater physical strength, they have been able to dominate and subjugate women. Even in the area of religion and spirituality, women were usually viewed as being inferior.

Then Jesus appeared. He introduced a radically different way of relating to women. When He spoke to women about God, He did so in exactly the same manner as to men. He always treated women with honor and respect. It was the women who followed Him to the cross and lingered below, while the men hid themselves in fear. It was to the women, and Mary Magdalene in particular, He first appeared to after His resurrection. They were the first to believe in His resurrection, while His disciples remained skeptical and fearful.

It was Paul who gave the clearest pronouncement on the place of women in the family of God when he wrote, "There is neither Jew nor Greek, slave nor free, male nor female, for you are all one in Christ Jesus" (Galatians 3:28).

Granted, there are differing roles and responsibilities, positions and offices, in which God has chosen to place the different sexes. They have different strengths and dispositions. But when it comes to knowing God, having a personal relationship with the Savior, God is blind to sexual differences. Both men and women are equal heirs of eternity.

There is a story in Matthew which illustrates this clearly. It reads as follows:

> That same day the Sadducees, who say there is no resurrection, came to him with a question. "Teacher," they said, "Moses told us that if a man dies without having children, his brother must marry the widow and have children for him. Now there were seven brothers among us. The first one married and died, and since he had no children, he left his wife to his brother. The same thing happened to the second and third brothers, right on down to the seventh. Finally, the woman died. Now then, at the resurrection, whose wife will she be of the seven, since all of them were married to her?" Jesus replied, "You are in error because you do not know the Scriptures or the power of God. At the resurrection people will neither marry nor be given in marriage; they will be like the angels in heaven (Matthew 22:23-30).

Some have misread this final phrase and assumed that we will become angels when we get to heaven. What Jesus said was, in regard to sex and marriage, we are going to be "like the angels." Angels are sexless. Sexuality is a purely earthly dynamic. In heaven, people's earthly sexual differences will no longer be identifiable. We will all be children of the Father; we will all be "sons of God."

Co-laborers

I believe there is still more inferred here by Peter. I believe that my wife is going to share equally in the fruits of my labors. My wife is not a teacher. She does not possess those kinds of ministry gifts. But she has been a vital source of support, insight and encouragement to my ministry as a pastor and teacher. I am convinced that she will have an equal share in the rewards and fruits of my teaching and pastoral ministry. We have a joint account. Whenever her heavenly balance grows, so does mine, and vice-versa.

We share in one another's fruits. We are equal partners. When I treat her with that kind of respect, she is encouraged and strengthened. She labors more heartily in our partnership. She comes to recognize the mutual benefit. She no longer sees herself competing with my ministry for my time, because it is no longer "my" ministry but "our" ministry.

Often men fail to recognize this vital connection. They separate their business or professional lives from their married lives. They don't see the critical support a wife can provide in helping her husband maintain balance professionally. She has more at stake than any other person in the world. She wants her husband to succeed, and yearns for an opportunity to participate with him in his career goals.

Yet men often shut their wives out of this area of their lives. They fail to share their burdens, to seek their perspective, advice and counsel. In so doing, men cut themselves off from one of their most valuable advisers. This woman not only knows her husband better than anyone else, she not only cares about him more than anyone else, but God has given her a unique perspective to empower her to be his "help-meet." To neglect such an asset is just plain stupid.

If you are wise, you will begin to inform her and include her in your "work" life. Ask her for her advice and for her prayers. It may take her a while to understand all the subtle aspects of what you do, but over time, she will grow in her grasp of your life's challenge. God will speak through her to you in ways that no one else will be able.

In Proverbs 31, Solomon speaks about the "virtuous" or noble woman. This is not a woman who is uninvolved. He portrays her as a craftsman, artisan, business person, farmer, manager. She is industrious, frugal, generous and gracious.

There are also some very revealing comments about her husband. Specifically, Solomon tells us two things about his attitude toward this virtuous woman:

1. "Her husband has full confidence in her . . ."(Proverbs 31:11).
2. He gives "her the reward she has earned, and let her works bring her praise at the city gate" (Proverbs 31:31).

Does this describe your attitude? Do you show "full confidence in her"? When she makes suggestions, or shares her concerns about a decision or direction, do you listen with thoughtful consideration?

In what ways do you reward your wife for all of her faithful support ? Do you make an effort to bless her for her sacrifices?

Do you ever praise her works "at the city gate"? When was the last time you bragged about your wife? Have you praised her publicly?

Most men I know, after having read this passage in Proverbs, are quick to point out the ways which their wives do not fulfill this description of virtue. I have a question for those men: What are you doing to encourage her to become this kind of woman? If you place your confidence in her, if you reward her and praise her publicly, she will strive to be a woman of virtue. But if you treat her as if she is incapable of understanding your burdens, if you rarely compliment her, if you rarely speak about her virtues publicly to others, she will soon become discouraged.

Through the years, I have known a few women who have become deeply virtuous, despite the failure of their husbands to honor them. But most women, deprived of their husbands' trust and praise, slowly wither away into discouragement. They crave their husbands' praise, but they never seem to do enough to gain it.

Many assume that it's due to some inadequacy within themselves—but that is rarely the case. Most often, men simply neglect to do what they should because they are too self-focused.

If this describes you, it's time to "wake-up and smell the coffee."

Adding Value

In some countries, there is a form of taxation called "added value." The idea is that at each stage in the manufacture of a product, the improvements made add value to the product. A tax is added to the resale of this product as it passes through each stage of the manufacturing process.

For example, a lumber company sells logs to a lumber mill. A tax is paid on the logs. The lumber company cuts the logs into finished lumber and sells it to a furniture manufacturer. Again a tax is added. At each stage of the manufacturing process, it is assumed that the value of the product has been increased. A tax is placed upon this increase.

Recently, I was attending a potluck at the home of one of my church leaders. While sitting in his living room, I noticed a couple of carved ducks which were done with amazing skill. They were the most beautifully carved ducks I have ever seen. They were done with exacting detail, down to the pin feathers.

When you think about it, the most amazing part is how those ducks started out. They were once just a block of wood. Their value was very small. Through skill and energy being applied to the wood, it had become something hundreds of times more valuable than it was in the beginning. Value had been added!

This is similar to what God seeks to do in each of our lives. We are born into this world with tremendous potential. We each have a brain and a body and the ability to develop intellectually, physically and spiritually. Yet not all of us reach the limits of our potential. We may be limited by our social environment and education. We may suffer from health problems. If we have never been exposed to the Gospel, we cannot grow spiritually. We have not been reborn of the Spirit.

There is also the issue of individual will. Today we hear a great deal about victimization. In some ways, we all are victims of someone or something, at sometime. But the greatest barrier to personal growth is our unwillingness to do what it takes to grow and change.

It is estimated that it takes 20,000 hours to become an expert at something. Ironically, the average child will spend that amount of time watching TV between the ages of three and 18 years. Thus, most kids become experts in watching TV. Unfortunately, such expertise is not in much demand and doesn't pay very well.

Most of us lack discipline, self-control and the willingness to do the hard work necessary to reach our goals in life. This is true for Christians as well as non-Christians. And it is especially true with regard to spiritual growth. We don't allow God to "add value" to our lives. Why? We don't like the way He does it. We hate the process.

How did the wooden ducks become "value-added"? By submitting the wood to the knife and allowing the needless parts to be cut away.

How does God "cut away" our needless parts? Through trials and testings. That is why James exhorts "Consider it pure joy, my brothers, whenever you face trials of many kinds" (James 1:2). I have met very few Christians who consistently view life's hardships from this point of view.

The potter and his clay

In several places in the Old and New Testaments (Isaiah 29:16; Isaiah 41:25; Isaiah 64:8; Jeremiah 18:4; Jeremiah 18:6; Romans 9:21), God describes his relationship with man in "value added" terms. He is the potter, we are the clay. He calls us to be supple and responsive to His shaping and molding of our lives, and as we do, our lives take on a shape which is honoring to Him and rewarding to us.

An added dimension of this process is the ability which God gives to us to add value to others, even as He adds value to us. When Paul wrote, "Therefore I urge you to imitate me . . . . Follow my example, as I follow the example of Christ" (1 Corinthians 4:16; 11:1), he was speaking of the capacity we possess to mentor others. By our example, we can provide a model of what God can do in the lives of those who are surrendered to Him. Again Paul explains it this way:

> Praise be to the God and Father of our Lord Jesus Christ, the Father of compassion and the God of all comfort, who comforts us in all our troubles, so that we can comfort those in any trouble with the comfort we ourselves have received

from God. For just as the sufferings of Christ flow over into our lives, so also through Christ our comfort overflows (2 Corinthians 1:3-5).

Although God wants us to find our primary role model and source of comfort in Christ, He also created us to be influenced by the actions and attitudes of others. In turn, He wants us to behave in a way which will encourage others to become more like Christ as well.

This is the means by which we "add value" to others. God adds value to us, and we in turn add value to others. Husbands are to treat their wives in a manner which adds value to them. We do this by being "considerate," "respectful," "supportive," "protective," and so forth. But the most effective way is through prayer—prayer for your spouse and with her.

> Husbands, in the same way be considerate . . . so that nothing will hinder your prayers (1 Peter 3:7).

Unfortunately, we often think we can change people to become the way we think they should be. In reality, there is very little that can be done to change other people. We can encourage people to allow the change to progress, once they have decided that they want to change. But only God can truly change a person, and that comes through the power and inward working of the Holy Spirit.

If you want to truly "add value" to another person, you need to commit to praying for them. This is the surest and most effective means of impacting another person's life for good.

I am convinced that when we get to heaven, the one question the angels are going to ask most of us is "Why didn't you pray more?" Prayer is the means by which a Christian can unlock the power of the universe. As the well known hymn "Trust and Obey" states, "Oh, what joy we often forfeit, oh what needless pain we bear . . . all because we do not carry everything to God in prayer."

Why is it that we are so delinquent in prayer? I suspect it is due to our desire to be in control. When my children were smaller, they would see me cutting the lawn. They would come out and ask if they could run the lawn mower. I knew they were too small to control the lawn mower, but I would let them try. I knew if I told them they were too young, too small, not strong enough—even though that was true—they still would pester me until I let them have a try at it. After a few short minutes, they would become tired and let me know that I could take over. When they were older and stronger, then they had to be commanded to run the lawn mower. It was no longer a challenge but a labor and a burden.

It works much the same way between us and God. We all want to be in control. We hate to admit that we aren't. I believe this is especially true for men. Have you ever noticed how difficult it is for men to ask for directions when they are lost—or to even admit that they are lost—when it is evident to everyone else? We just have difficulty admitting to ourselves and others that we aren't in control of the situation.

So God allows us to try it on our own. He sits back and watches us exhaust ourselves. He patiently waits for us to turn to Him and say, "You can take control again. It's too much for me."

The very posture of prayer is an acknowledgement that the issues before us are too great for us to handle. Once the child of God comes to the point of acknowledgement, God more than takes over. He shows His strength and power in every area of our lives. We move from defeat to victory in a moment—the moment of surrender!

Hindered prayer

There is nothing more disastrous in the Christian life than "hindered prayer." Without prayer, we become like soldiers deprived of their weapons. We are unable to stand against our enemies.

Peter closed the seventh verse of his first letter with a strong warning: "Husbands, in the same way be considerate . . . so that nothing will hinder your prayers" (1 Peter 3:7). What is it that hinders prayer? The Bible identifies only one culprit: Sin! When men fail to treat their wives properly, in God's eyes they are in sin—willful, habitual, continual rebellion against God.

When sin is allowed to reign in our lives, God will not do

the things we desire. We become unable to fulfill the purposes for which God has called us. We become blocked and frustrated in all our doings. Life goes backward instead of forward.

There are two things that every man should commit to do: 1. Pray for his wife, and 2. Pray with his wife. I believe this will do more for a marriage and family than any combination of things a man can attempt. Why? Paul supplies a clear answer in the letters of 2 Corinthians and Ephesians:

> For though we live in the world, we do not wage war as the world does. The weapons we fight with are not the weapons of the world. On the contrary, they have divine power to demolish strongholds. We demolish arguments and every pretension that sets itself up against the knowledge of God, and we take captive every thought to make it obedient to Christ (2 Corinthians 10:3-5).

> Finally, be strong in the Lord and in his mighty power. Put on the full armor of God so that you can take your stand against the devil's schemes. For our struggle is not against flesh and blood, but against the rulers, against the authorities, against the powers of this dark world and against the spiritual forces of evil in the heavenly realms .... And pray in the Spirit on all occasions with all kinds of prayers and requests. With this in mind, be alert and always keep on praying for all the saints (Ephesians 6:10-18).

The power of prayer

As mentioned earlier, at several different places in Scripture, the Lord refers to our relationship with Him as being like that of a potter to his clay. He is constantly kneading us, casting us upon the wheel, shaping and molding us after the purpose of His will. For each and every one of us, He has a unique and artful design. Each has a specific purpose for which our lives are shaped and formed.

In most of the references listed above, God is having a problem with the clay. It is unwilling to accept the design He has intended. Ironically, the clay is resisting its master, the potter. The metaphor is ridiculous, but then, so is the reality it seeks to portray—to think that we should be so bold as to resist the plan of God for our lives. Yet, that is the way it usually is. Why?

Most of the time we are too concerned with being "right" and proving it. We strive to be in control and are too proud to admit our weaknesses. Therefore, God must re-knead the clay and throw us again and again on the wheel, until we begin to respond to His shaping hands.

When we pray, the process goes much more quickly and smoothly. It is prayer which makes the clay supple and responsive to the Master. Prayer is the means by which we become "conformable" (Philippians 3:10) to His will.

I learned this lesson early in my married life. As I have shared before, my wife and I had a deeply troubled marriage in the beginning. I remember so well praying one day that God would convict and correct her for not treating me with respect, for not trusting in my leadership. "Make her submit," was the essence of my prayer. Yet as I prayed, I felt my prayers were not being heard. All I was doing was ventilating my feelings. There was no real communication taking place between God and me. I sensed no comfort or confidence that God was hearing my pleas. Slowly, I began to quiet myself before Him. I asked, "Lord if there is something that needs to change in me, I am willing to hear about it."

In a moment, my disposition changed from anger to heaviness. It suddenly became so apparent, so obvious. I saw the hardness and bitterness of my heart. Pride and selfishness began to crawl out from under the covers of my anger. In a moment, I was pleading with God to forgive me and have mercy upon me. How could I complain about my wife's behavior when there was such ugliness in my heart? What was there in me that would encourage her to trust and respect me?

This proved to be a major turning point in our relationship. It may have saved our marriage. The path I needed to follow became crystal clear. The issue was no longer about her becoming the right kind of wife or of remaking her into the person I wanted her to be. The issue was me growing in my walk with God, so I could "become" the right kind of husband.

Pray for your wife

When was the last time you prayed for your wife? I didn't ask, "When was the last time you prayed 'about' your wife?" Rather, when was the last time you specifically spent some time interceding for your wife's welfare and blessing? This is something you should be doing daily.

One of the areas of greatest deception is that we can change another person. We can't change anyone, really. Only God can change a heart, and that through the process of repentance.

Repentance comes through God alone. Paul declared as much: ". . . God's kindness leads you toward repentance" (Romans 2:4).

When a husband or wife nag and criticize his or her spouse into changing an area of behavior, the spouse may make every effort to stop doing whatever it is that is offensive, especially if the behavior causes a strong, negative reaction from their mate. Because the change is only outward and not from the heart, the relationship begins to die inwardly, even while the outward behavior is conforming. Eventually, the offending party learns how to avoid conflict. It becomes like navigating through a mine field. What suffers is communication that leads to intimacy and trust. One begins to live in fear of offending. Whenever the "other" is present, you become *en garde*, careful not to do or say anything that would lead to conflict.

In the final analysis, there has not been a changed heart. Consequently, the offending behavior is only suppressed, not resolved. Guilt has replaced love as the motivator. Over time, guilt gives way to anger and resentment.

At the same time, the mate who is complaining also becomes dissatisfied. He or she senses the resentment. He or she knows that the changes are only superficial. He or she feels accused and misunderstood.

I remember too well how this worked between my wife and me. She complained that I never showed her that I was thinking of her through the day. I never called or brought her flowers or candy just to surprise her. So what was my response? I put it on my "to do" list. I called; I bought candy; I brought flowers home. To my chagrin, she still complained. She rightly stated, "You're only doing it because you have to."

When I stepped back and examined my motives, I discovered that she was right. I had interpreted her complaints to be performance expectations, just like I did on the job. My gifts and phone calls were not the spontaneous expressions of loving and caring. They were "duty"!

But I was without a clue how to change. I didn't have an example from watching my parents as a child. There was little sincere affection and love expressed. Gifts were always very practical and never spontaneous.

Over time, my wife stopped complaining and began praying for me. I also began to pray that the Lord would help me hear what my wife was saying to me. I have learned that my wife needs to know that she is important to me 24 hours a day. She needs to know that I yearn to bless her and to show her signs of my love. This is my "duty" to her. I can't put it on my calendar or "to do" list. It has to come from the heart, freely, sincerely, and spontaneously.

Even Jesus

Jesus expressed similar dissatisfaction when He told the Pharisees that they drew near to God with their words but their hearts were somewhere else (Matthew 15:8). They weren't in love with God. They feared Him. They sought to appease Him or manipulate Him to fulfill or justify their selfish desires. If they made changes in their behavior, it was due only to fear or prudence, not loving actions. If there are behaviors you dislike in your spouse, then pray for him or her. Don't just pray that God would change his or her behavior. Pray that God would draw your spouse close to Himself; to enrich his or her fellowship with the Savior; to open the wonders of His Word to your spouse's heart; to create an insatiable hunger for His Word and Will in his or her life.

God will always honor such praying, for this is His desire, His perfect will for your partner in life (and for you as well). As we draw near to the Lord, we will increasingly take on the likeness of His nature, being "conformed to the image of His Son," (Romans 8:29, KJV). The change will come slowly, but surely. It will happen from the inside out. The results are not as sudden, but they are more sure, more meaningful and lasting.

Pray together

It used to surprise me how many couples find it difficult to pray together. As I investigated this problem further, it began to make sense. True praying requires "harmony." Jesus put it this way: "Again, I tell you that if two of you on earth agree about anything you ask for, it will be done for you by my Father in heaven" (Matthew 18:19).

The transliteration of the word "agree" is *sumphoneo* (*sum*, together, *phone*, a sound). It means "to be in accord, primarily of musical instruments."[21] It is the root of our English word, symphony.

When two believers pray with their hearts in agreement, it produces a heavenly harmony in the heart of God, more beautiful than any earthly orchestra could ever produce. That is why God delights in our praying. But the key to successful group prayer is harmony, or agreement.

Unresolved issues

There is never a time when we are more transparent than when we pray sincerely from our hearts. I have found that couples who have difficulty praying together are having trouble trusting one another with that much vulnerability. When people are guarded about showing their true heart feelings, praying doesn't work. Yet, as I have stated before, prayer is the only key that can open the doors of greater blessing upon your marriage. Remember, Jesus promised that if we do agree, "anything you ask for, it will be done for you by my Father in heaven." The need for answered prayer is the motivator that pushes us past our fear of being vulnerable and transparent and opens the doors of blessing in marriage.

Let me give you another example from my marriage. My wife and I had been married for about five years when I began to recognize the signs of minor depression in her behavior. Not knowing how to deal with her struggle, I sought out counsel from a friend who was experienced in marital counseling. He suggested that my wife and I begin setting aside time each night to talk, read the Bible and pray together.

At first it was pretty painful. When I asked her to share with me anything that I might be doing to contribute to her depression, it was like opening a flood gate. I had to bite my lip. I had no idea there were so many things that I was doing, and wasn't doing, that were upsetting to her.

After what seemed like an eternity, she finally stopped sharing. We then read a chapter out of Proverbs and prayed. I asked the Lord to forgive me and help me to be more sensitive to my wife's needs. She prayed for forgiveness for her bitterness against me.

We continued to spend this time together each night for several months. Slowly we both began to grow and change. Our sharing time slowly became less charged. Eventually it became a wonderful time of fellowship and affirmation. The Word came alive to us as we experienced God's ministry to our hearts. We started a prayer list, citing the supplication, the date it was entered, and the date it was fulfilled. Our faith grew as we saw God heal our marriage and build our faith as He answered one prayer after another. There was not a single request that He did not answer, not a single need He failed to fulfill.

We still have that old prayer journal. Once in a while we come across it. What a wonderful testimony it has become to us of the power of God and the efficacy of prayer.

If you and your spouse can't pray together, try doing what my wife and I did, or come up with a program of your own. What is most important is that you not allow Satan to rob you of such a powerful avenue of blessing. Put aside your pride and hurt feelings. Invite the Spirit of the Lord to bring blessing and liberty into your home through praying regularly together.

9

Men Who Will Not Lead!

In the Lord, however, woman is not independent of man, nor is man independent of woman. For as woman came from man, so also man is born of woman. But everything comes from God. Judge for yourselves: Is it proper for a woman to pray to God with her head uncovered? Does not the very nature of things teach you that if a man has long hair, it is a disgrace to him, but that if a woman has long hair, it is her glory? For long hair is given to her as a covering. If anyone wants to be contentious about this, we have no other practice —nor do the churches of God (1 Corinthians 11:3-16).

When something goes wrong, we want to know, "Who is responsible?" When we have a complaint, we want to know, "Who is in charge?"

A fundamental understanding that we all have about our world is that someone has to be in charge; someone has to be responsible. When no one is in charge, there is chaos. Whether we are talking about government, business, athletics, the church, the family, whatever, there has to be someone who is responsible to make sure things operate properly. When things go wrong, there has to be someone who can give direction, take charge, provide solutions. That is why we have policemen, firemen, mayors, governors, soldiers, presidents, mechanics. These are people to whom we have given delegated authority to be in charge of specific areas of need. That is also why families have husbands and fathers.

Headship

As with everything else, so also in the family, someone has to be in charge. Under the biblical design, the man is to be the leader and final authority in the home. The Apostle Paul explained the chain of authority this way: "Now I want you to realize that the head of every man is Christ, and the head of the woman is man, and the head of Christ is God (1 Corinthians 11:3). It is a simple pyramid of delegated authority that looks like this:

```
                    /\
                   /  \
                  /    \
                 / GOD  \
                / CHRIST \
               /HUSBAND/FATHER\
              / WIFE/MOTHER \
             /  CHILDREN    \
            /_____\
```

When it comes to marriage and the family, God has ordained that the man is to provide primary leadership. Ultimately, he is the one responsible for everything that happens within the family. In Bible terms, it is called headship.

Families are not democracies. As Paul describes them, they are to be theocracies! They are to be governed by God. He has set up a very concise system of authority through which the family is to be governed.

God the Father has given authority to Christ His Son. Biblically, Christ is identified as the "head" of the church, which is His body (Ephesians 5:23; Colossians 1:18; 2:19). In turn, Christ has delegated authority to the husband/father to model Christ-like leadership in the home. The wife/mother is to submit to her husband as the church is submitted unto Christ (Ephesians 5:22). Lastly, children are to honor their parents (Colossians 3:20). Each family member has a role to fulfill; a role which God has ordained specifically for them. Not everyone in an Indian tribe could be chief. Not everyone in the family can be in charge. God has reserved that position for the man.

Back to the garden

Some have speculated that before Adam and Eve sinned our two original parents were on equal footing in all things. That is not what Scripture teaches: "For the man is not of the woman; but the woman of the man. Neither was the man created for the woman; but the woman for the man" (1 Corinthians 11:8,9).

From the very beginning of His creation, God intended for the man to be first in leadership and responsibility. That is why, Paul explained, He created man first, then woman.

I realize that some will take issue with this principle. Paul must have anticipated your objections, for he concludes his discussion by stating, "If anyone wants to be contentious about this, we have no other practice—nor do the churches of God" (1 Corinthians 11:16.) In other words, the principle is inviolable. This is the only pattern God will honor.

Granted, in many ways, a marriage is really a partnership—a partnership between a husband and wife. But even in partnerships there is need for a "senior" partner. Most partnerships fail because people realize too late the need for clear lines of authority, the need for one partner to be the final decision maker.

Gentle leaders

When a family is functioning in the manner which God designed it, the leadership of the husband is expressed silently, gently and lovingly. He leads from the strength and the confidence inherent in his God-given role as the leader of his home. As such, he is the servant-leader of his home, even as Jesus modeled servant-leadership during His earthly ministry. He summarized the principle by stating, "The greatest among you will be your servant" (Matthew 23:11).

We used to refer to government employees as "public servants," because their job was to serve the public. We, the people, have given them delegated authority to govern, to protect, to defend and to serve the citizens of the land.

Husbands, similarly, are to be "family servants." Just as God has ordained that governments should rule nations

(Romans 13:1-7), so also He has ordained that husbands and fathers should rule in the home. The motive should be of serving, not the raw exercise of power over others.

When a man is running around, raising his voice, using threats, manipulation and coercion to hold on to control, he is missing the point completely. He is trying to assert his leadership rather than allowing God to manifest his leadership. He has not yet grasped that the purpose of godly leadership is not to control but to serve, not just to rule but also to bless, care for and protect.

The example of Joshua

When Joshua was elevated by God to take the place of Moses, he was stepping into a mighty big pair of shoes. The people agreed to follow him as their leader, but there was a stipulation: "Just as we fully obeyed Moses, so we will obey you. Only may the LORD your God be with you as He was with Moses" (Joshua 1:17). This was a pretty conditional commitment. They were saying, "We will give you the benefit of the doubt for now. But you're going to have to prove that you are really God's chosen one."

A lesser man would have begun to scheme how he was going to prove his worth, but Joshua left promotion in God's hands. After all, it was God who had "raised him up," and it was God who would make him successful. Listen to the promise the Lord gave Joshua: "And the LORD said to Joshua, 'Today I will begin to exalt you in the eyes of all Israel, so that they may know that I am with you as I was with Moses'" (Joshua 3:7).

How did God fulfill His word? He parted the waters of the Jordan while they were at flood stage, and Israel walked across on dry ground. Listen to what follows in the sacred record: "That day the LORD exalted Joshua in the sight of all Israel; and they revered him all the days of his life, just as they had revered Moses" (Joshua 4:14). They not only respected him, they "revered" him!

All that Joshua had to do was listen for God's voice and obey His commands. In fact, if Joshua had tried to figure out how to prove himself, he would have been too preoccupied to listen for God's direction.

Gentlemen, do not fall into the trap of trying to prove through human strength or ability that God has called you to be the head of your family. Even if no one else believes it, it is God's ordained ideal. It is a fact of life. Focus on being faithful to the Lord, and He will establish your family around the principles of His Word.

You can expect that when you begin to walk in this new role, you will encounter opposition. Satan doesn't want you behaving like a godly man. He doesn't want God's best for you and your family. He is going to do everything he can to discourage and dissuade you from your commitment to become a godly husband and father.

Opposition may come from those you love the most—your wife and children. This is extremely painful for a man to endure. But don't give up. Rather, accept it as God's will for your life. If you are humbled, embarrassed—if your feelings are hurt—it's happening because that is what needs to happen in your life to make you into the man that God wants you to be. If your wife and children dishonor you, don't become angry or depressed. Instead, rejoice, knowing that you are bearing the sufferings of Christ. Paul counted such a circumstance to be an opportunity for boasting: "That is why, for Christ's sake, I delight in weaknesses, in insults, in hardships, in persecutions, in difficulties. For when I am weak, then I am strong" (2 Corinthians 12:10).

As you continue to faithfully follow the Lord's will, He will change the hearts of those who resist you. He will give you favor within your family by demonstrating His calling upon your life to be the head of your home.

Let me give you two passages of Scripture to hang on to until that happens:

> Let us not become weary in doing good, for at the proper time we will reap a harvest if we do not give up (Galatians 6:9).

> Therefore, my dear brothers, stand firm. Let nothing move you. Always give yourselves fully to the work of the Lord, because you know that your labor in the Lord is not in vain (1 Corinthians 15:58).

Go slowly

Let me offer another caution. Go slowly! Whenever you are contemplating making a major life change, live with it in your own thought-life for a long time, before you try to apply it to those around you.

As a pastor, I have learned this lesson the hard way. Early in my ministry, I would attend a conference or seminar. I would hear some new way of doing ministry. It sounded great, so I would begin to implement changes as soon as I got home. I was always shocked when my people would resist or react negatively. I would accuse them of resisting God, not listening to the Lord, being rebellious.

Over the years, I have learned that I was being unfair to those good people. I hadn't even learned to live what I was wanting them to live. I hadn't given God the opportunity to show me whether or not this was even His will for our church.

Many of those people got very angry at me. I am sure some of them are still angry. And it's my fault. If what I was trying to do was really of the Lord, He would have begun to reveal it to them over time, even as He had revealed it to me. In the same way, your wife and children may not immediately accept you in this new leadership role, especially if you have not, up until now, been faithful in providing leadership and serving their needs before your own. They are not accustomed to you taking on some of the responsibilities and showing interest and concern in areas which you have neglected in the past. They have adapted to doing many things themselves, no longer looking to you for leadership and support.

So go slowly. Let the Lord give evidence of your leadership. Let the Lord demonstrate to them that they are safe in submitting to your rule. Approach the role as Jesus did when He appeared on earth to men. Your attitude should be the same as that of Christ Jesus:

> Who, being in very nature God, did not consider equality with God something to be grasped, but made himself nothing, taking the very nature of a servant, being made in human likeness. And being found in appearance as a man, he humbled himself and became obedient to death —even death

on a cross! Therefore God exalted him to the highest place and gave him the name that is above every name, that at the name of Jesus every knee should bow, in heaven and on earth and under the earth (Philippians 2:5-10).

Jesus possessed all the power and authority of heaven and earth. He came to rule over His kingdom—the hearts of men—but His purpose was to "win" the hearts of men, not take control of their bodies. Therefore, He "made Himself nothing, taking the very nature of a servant," and "He humbled Himself." What was the result? "Therefore God exalted Him to the highest place and gave Him the name that is above every name." Remember, as you humble yourself, God will exalt you, too (Matthew 23:12; 1 Peter 5:6).

Men who won't lead

In many marriages today, there are two problems which have undermined the divine design for the family: 1. Husbands who won't lead, and 2. Wives who will not follow. It has produced frustrated men, angry women and children who no longer respect the authority structure of the family.

Why is this? I believe that it is due in large degree to the confusion over male and female roles. Men and women both are unsure as to how they are supposed to relate to one another. Men are often intimidated out of fulfilling male roles. Women are fearful to let them.

How did we get into this state of affairs? Our parents didn't seem to have such a difficult time knowing where their place was. They took it for granted that men and women were different. They accepted that the difference was the result of God's creative design. They were not shocked when men expressed different interests than women or reacted to situations differently. For the most part, their acceptance and submission to the differences enabled them to move on with the business of life without guilt or confusion. They delighted in the differences rather than viewing them as the battlefield of life.

But in the late 1960s, a new tide of thinking began to express itself. With Darwinian evolution as the basis of their thinking, a group of social activists began asserting that men and women were essentially the same. They posited that if you were to place boys and girls in exactly the same environment, with identical stimulus, they would turn out to be identical in behavior and attitude. Areas like math and science, government and corporate leadership, would soon be populated by as many women as men; maybe more! After all, as many were fond of saying, "The best man for the job is a woman!"

Today, we now know that there are profound and inherent differences between the sexes that go as deep as our DNA molecules. George Gilder, in the original groundbreaking work, Men and Marriage, summing up the consensus of scientific evidence, stated:

> The ultimate vision of the sexual liberationist: the two sexes are essentially identical, inessentially and arbitrarily divided. To most people over the centuries this view would have seemed preposterous. And so it is today. For after all these years, scientists are finally affirming what nonexperts have always known: that there are profound and persistent biological differences between the sexes, with which every society must come to terms . . . from conception to maturity, men and women are subjected to different hormonal influences that shape their bodies, brains, and temperaments in different ways . . . . The sexes become significantly different, even in the very organization of their brains, during the time in the womb.[22]

At our very human core, our brains are structured differently, which in turn controls the difference in the ways men and women think, act, and react to life's situations. Because of these differences, each sex brings vastly different capacities to the table of life.

Those who would claim otherwise fit into the category outlined by the Apostle Paul in Romans:

> For although they knew God, they neither glorified him as God nor gave thanks to him, but their thinking became futile and their foolish hearts were darkened. Although they claimed to be wise, they became fools (Romans 1:21, 22).

Unfortunately, most men and women are still operating under the old ideas. These activists were able to promote their ideas long enough and loudly enough that they succeeded in convincing an entire generation of something that is absolutely untrue.

It is time for many of us to start behaving as we were designed by God, without guilt or apology. Men are men, and women are women, and so shall it ever be.

Neglect?

Because of this confusion over roles, and the increasing emphasis upon personal fulfillment, it has become common for men to abandon their God-given responsibilities. Instead of providing leadership and carrying the weight of family responsibilities, they choose to ignore or run away from them.

In some cases, men have simply disappeared, leaving a wife and children to fend for themselves. But a more typical form of desertion is called abdication. In such cases, a man may be physically present but withdraws to the point where the woman is forced to take over leadership and decision-making roles most of the time.

I characterize this kind of abdication as emotional neglect. It happens when a man becomes so involved in his own narrowly defined agenda that he ignores, or neglects, the pressing needs of his wife and family. This robs his wife of the sense of protection and provision that is essential for her sense of well being. This often becomes the catalyst for nagging and nit-picking, of which men complain so often.

Dear John

It is intriguing to me how many husbands will come home one evening to an empty house, with only a "Dear John" letter to notify them of a wife's departure. They are stunned and disoriented. Were there no clues, no signs, no indication of what was happening?

Whenever I have probed, I have found plenty of indicators. There were threats, short separations, attempts at counseling, books and pamphlets left on reading tables—all to no avail. The poor guy had just tuned out anything that was unpleasant.

Finally, his once-loving bride decided the frustration was too much. "It's easier to go it alone than to face the pain of isolation any more," I have heard them say. "What difference does it make? I have been living alone for years. Now there will be fewer dirty clothes and dishes to wash."

I am in no way advocating or recommending the above response. I've just seen it too many times. These women may be giving up too quickly. It seems the tolerance level for women is getting lower and lower. More women are less willing to endure a difficult situation, but that doesn't excuse the man. He must face his failures squarely, like a man.

These men are not stupid people. It's just that none of us have eyes in the backs of our heads. If we are facing in the wrong direction, if we neglect what is going on around us, we will miss even the most obvious signs. Sometimes it's due to ignorance and sometimes denial, but in the end, it comes out to be the same thing—neglect. People can get so wrapped up in "things," they fail to pay attention to all that is going wrong in the most important area of their lives.

Managing the home

Abdicating husbands are usually guilty of unwittingly "neglecting" key family responsibilities. When Paul set out to delineate the qualifications of spiritual leaders in 1 Timothy, much of what he had to say revolved around a man's home life. In particular, Paul declared, "He must manage his own family well and see that his children obey him with proper respect. (If anyone does not know how to manage his own family, how can he take care of God's church?)" (1 Timothy 3:4, 5).

There is an obvious inference that can be drawn from Paul's words: Management requires attention. The Greek word we translate "to manage" (*proistemi*) means "to be over, to superintend, preside over, to be a protector or guardian, to give aid, to care for, give attention to." This is no casual endeavor. It requires concerted focus and energy. It requires one to take the task with the highest level of seriousness.

Why is this true regarding the family? Marriages and families do not grow themselves. Strong, happy, healthy, successful homes are the consequence of husbands, wives, mothers, fathers who have purposefully chosen to do those things which will bring about positive results (Proverbs 22:6). Conversely, unhealthy marriages and families are the consequence of neglect.

This should be obvious to us. We see it all around us. When the favorite past-time and primary source of information and culturization is television (as it is in most homes), both marriages and families will become emotionally, intellectually and spiritually undernourished. It's like never changing the oil in your car. It will run for an amazingly long time, but eventually, the internal corruption of dirty oil will damage your engine and decrease its effectiveness. Families, like cars, tend to break down and fail at the most critical times, when we need them to be at their strongest. Why? Because these are times of high stress, when our weakest links reveal how strong or weak we really are.

Most of us already know this, but we haven't acted upon what we know. We're too busy doing other things. We have careers to build, projects to complete, money to make, vacations to plan, ball games to watch, hobbies to perfect, ad nauseum. For each, it may be something different, and therefore, we conclude that we are different. But in the end, the same results come. Too many of us live in houses occupied by roommates instead of families.

A matter of right priorities

I have often been challenged and comforted by the Lord's words to Jonah, especially as it is expressed in the King James: "They that observe lying vanities forsake their own mercy" (Jonah 2:8, KJV). This has always seemed an apt description of the major problem most of us face. We are often misled, seduced into pursuing the wrong things. We lean our ladder up against a wall and spend a major portion of our lives trying to climb to the top. When we finally get there, we realize that we have scaled the wrong wall. Our priorities have been all wrong.

Today, making right choices, keeping our priorities in right order, is much more difficult than in the past. More and more, our free time is being eliminated. What free time we have is bombarded with media images and messages, all claiming to be of critical importance. They contradict or challenge much of what we believe to be true. We are pulled in every direction. Most people I talk to can't clearly tell you where their life is headed. They simply live day to day. No plan, no strategy, no sense of calling or destiny.

Where are you headed?

Is it any wonder there are so few real leaders today. The adage is true: "If you don't know where you're going, you'll end up somewhere else." Jesus told us where that "somewhere else" is: "Let them alone: they be blind leaders of the blind. And if the blind lead the blind, both shall fall into the ditch" (Matthew 15:14, KJV).

Jesus' teachings are full of challenges to direct our lives rightly. We are told to build our house on the rock and not on the sand (Matthew 6:24-27), to seek first the kingdom of God and His righteousness (Matthew 6:33), that there is no profit if you gain the whole world and lose your soul (Matthew 16:26), and many other such references. He repeatedly challenges the Bible reader to make the right choices.

The questions each of us need to be asking ourselves over and over again are, "What is the controlling force in my life? What is my driving passion? What determines and dictates the way I spend my time, my energy, my money?"

Jesus has clearly declared what that right choice is:

> Do not store up for yourselves treasures on earth, where moth and rust destroy, and where thieves break in and steal. But store up for yourselves treasures in heaven, where moth and rust do not destroy, and where thieves do not break in and steal. For where your treasure is, there your heart will be also (Matthew 6:19-21).

Head knowledge vs. heart knowledge

When I ask most Christian men to tell me what their life priorities are, they usually can give me the right answer: God first, then my family, and lastly, my career. Those of us who have been around the church long enough have learned how we are supposed to answer such questions. Few of us actually follow these priorities.

Many years ago, I had a pastor from another community come to my office with his wife. They were seeking counsel for their marriage. They lived in a city 150 miles away. They had driven all that distance because they did not want anyone in their community or church to know that they were having marital difficulties.

I began talking with both of them, and after about an hour, I sensed resistance coming from the husband. I asked his wife to step out for a few minutes, and then I began to probe. As we talked, the man began deflecting my questions. And when I began to quote Scripture he snapped back at me: "I know what the Bible says about marriage. I've tried it and it doesn't work."

Here was a man who weekly was telling His congregation that the Bible was reliable, that they should base their lives on its teachings and follow it confidently and unerringly. Yet he questioned whether it worked in his marriage.

At first, I was taken aback by his response. Then I remembered when I had felt the same way some years earlier, but I had come to discover that the problem was with me, not the Bible.

You see, many of us know what the words of the Bible say, but we have never completely committed to fully following them. We hold back because we are afraid God's Word will fail us. As a consequence, we have never experienced it in its fullness.

God's Word becomes real to us when we allow it to prove itself in our lives, but this involves risk. That is the hard part about faith. Men and women of faith are risk-takers. They have risked the loss of everything to attain the fullness of Christ (Philippians 3:7-11).

I went on to share with this man what I had come to discover about myself: "You don't know what the Bible says. If you truly knew it, you would apply it. All you know about the Word of God is what you have put into your head. Only when you allow it to penetrate your heart will you be able to say that you truly know it, because you will have experienced its power through faith. Then you will know that it works."

Too many Christians mistakenly believe that because they are Christians, go to church and marry in a church theirs is a Christian marriage. Living in a garage doesn't make you a car. Going to church doesn't make you a Christian. And marrying a Christian, doesn't make it a Christian marriage. That only comes when you begin to apply biblical principles and priorities to your marriage.

Where do I start?

Most men realize that their most basic duty as a husband and father is to provide for their families. Unfortunately, they tend to define their role as providers very narrowly—they limit it to financial provision.

Certainly, meeting the financial needs of your family is important. Scripture tells us as much: "If anyone does not provide for his relatives, and especially for his immediate family, he has denied the faith and is worse than an unbeliever" (1 Timothy 5:8).

It would be accurate to say that this is where a man's giving and service to his family begins. But there is much more to being a provider than putting food on the table, clothes on our children's backs and a roof over their heads. A man also needs to provide spiritual leadership and emotional affirmation.

Spiritual leadership

Spiritual leadership should be the most important priority in a man's list of things he needs to provide for his family. Yet it is often the most neglected. In many families, men view spiritual things as being in the domain of women. Many connote spirituality with femininity.

Nothing could be further from the truth. One needs only to study the life of Jesus and the Apostles to realize that being spiritually minded is one of the most masculine attitudes a man can have. It takes great courage, because once a man decides to dedicate himself to God alone, he encounters innumerable challenges and great resistance.

Boundaries

When God brought the tribes of Israel into the land of Canaan, He told them what the boundaries of the nation were to be. They were to take possession of everything within those borders, but not beyond. In a similar manner He gave them social boundaries—laws, statutes, ordinances. These were the borders that were to control their attitudes and actions toward others.

Similarly, the New Testament gives the church boundaries. We are God's children, His purchased possessions, His bond-servants. We are His Kingdom, and our lives are to be about allowing more of ourselves to be conquered and absorbed into His heavenly Kingdom. The objective is not to "do" something for God, but to "become" more like Christ. Paul contrasts the two sides of this process in Romans:

> For whom He did foreknow, He also did predestinate to be conformed to the image of his Son, that He might be the firstborn among many brethren (Romans 8:29, KJV).

> And be not conformed to this world: but be ye trans-formed by the renewing of your mind, that ye may prove what is that good, and acceptable, and perfect, will of God (Romans 12:2, KJV).

Herein lies the challenge. We are to allow God to "conform" us to the image of His Son, while resisting the often more attractive option of being "conformed to this world."

In some ways it's an issue of significance. Where are you going to invest your time and energy to gain a sense of worth, value and significance? With whom or what are you going to identify? Who are going to be your heroes? Role models? Mentors? Who do you want to look like when you look in the mirror? Who are you striving to be when no one else is looking?

The Bible tells us that we should be concerned primarily with living a life that is pleasing to God.

> And we pray this in order that you may live a life worthy of the Lord and may please Him in every way: bearing fruit in every good work, growing in the knowledge of God (Colossians 1:10).

> On the contrary, we speak as men approved by God to be entrusted with the gospel. We are not trying to please men but God, who tests our hearts (1 Thessalonians 2:4).

Herein lies our greatest difficulty. For the most part, we are far more concerned with "trying to please men" than God. Our actions reveal the truth about what our true priorities are. We can make any claim we want, but "a tree is recognized by its fruit" (Matthew 12:33). What is your fruit?

Seek first the kingdom of God

Any discussion regarding a man's provision for his family must begin with spiritual leadership. Why? Because that is where Jesus said all things should begin: "But seek first His kingdom and His righteousness, and all these things (food, shelter, raiment) will be given to you as well" (Matthew 6:33).

This is the key to success in all life's arenas. God promises that if we focus upon seeking Him and His kingdom (will, purpose and plan), He will ensure that everything else that is needful for our lives will be provided. Consequently, His commitment to husbands and fathers is that if they provide spiritual leadership in their homes, He will meet all the other needs of their families as well. His blessing will flow out of their devotion to Christ.

Not surprisingly, this is where the greatest challenge comes. A basic fact of life is that it is easier to believe in the money I can see than in the invisible God whom I cannot see. If I am going to prioritize my life according to God's Word, I must walk by faith. I must trust that His Word is true.

Management of resources

Assuming that you have agreed with me so far and are motivated to put your life into its proper order, we need to move on to application. Basically, we are talking about the management of your resources. I only have three: my time, my money, and my energy. The most important of these is my time. Time is irreplaceable. Once spent, it is gone forever. Money in one sense is only compressed time. Like energy, it can increase the yield of my time because I can bring more labor to bear on my goal.

This, of course, leads us to the discussion about quality vs. quantity of time. It really isn't a very meaningful discussion. Good results in life require both. A quality product is the consequence of applying a quantity of time. When we are facing surgery, we have three questions for the surgeon:

1. Have you ever done this procedure before?
2. How many times?
3. What were the results?

All three questions are quantity plus quality questions.

If you are going to be an effective provider for your family, especially in spiritual and emotional terms, it is going to take time. God, through His Spirit and His Word, wants to retrain you in His ways. It is the same challenge which Paul gave to the Roman church when he wrote:

> Therefore, I urge you, brothers, in view of God's mercy, to offer your bodies as living sacrifices, holy and pleasing to God—this is your spiritual act of worship. Do not conform any longer to the pattern of this world, but be transformed by the renewing of your mind. Then you will be able to test and approve what God's will is—his good, pleasing and perfect will. For by the grace given me I say to every one of you: Do not think of yourself more highly than you ought, but rather think of yourself

with sober judgment, in accordance with the measure of
faith God has given you (Romans 12:1-3).

Making it a habit

Earlier, I mentioned that it takes 20,000 hours for a person
to become an "expert" at something. That is a massive quantity of time in human terms. You cannot become accomplished
in any area of your life until you are willing to dedicate ad-
equate amounts of time to its completion. It is time which makes
something a habit—doing the same thing over and over again,
until it becomes unthinking and effortless. That's what a habit
is.

Many of us are in the habit of being unspiritual, poor fathers and husbands. The models with which we grew up and
the examples we see all around us do not empower us to become effective spiritual leaders in our homes. It is going to
take a strong resolution and a long-term commitment to build
new spiritual habits.

The strength of a habit is determined by the frequency with
which it is repeated. If you set aside a time to pray and read
every day and follow through with your commitment, it will
take you about 39 days for it to become a regular habit. If you
hit or miss, it will take you somewhat longer. In fact, hit or
miss may become your new habit.

Take time for God

The question I am most often asked at this point is, "How
do I change?" The most important decision most men have to
make is whether or not they will surrender their schedule to
allow room for God and their family. If I really believe in my
heart what God is saying, I will begin to adjust my schedule
and ration my energy around meeting the spiritual needs of
my family first.

I will start by setting aside regular times for personal Bible
study and devotions. I will pray daily for the needs of my wife
and children, as well as for myself. I will involve my life with
other Christian men, through church services, Bible studies,

prayer meetings, home groups, men's fellowships, whatever. I will take every opportunity to seek spiritual "feeding."

As you do these things, you begin to discover ways to minister to your family. It will happen, not because you put it on your "to-do" list; rather, it will come as the overflow of your life in Christ. You will begin to lead spiritually in your home first by your own godly example, and then through the attitude of your heart and the words of your mouth.

I haven't got the time!

The protest I most often hear from men is, "I haven't got any more time to give!" That is probably true, as long as you are unwilling to give up other things. For many, it will require giving up something as simple as a hobby, or TV time. For others, it may mean a change of career.

We all live in the same universe. We each only have 24 hours per day. What separates us is how we decide to use those hours. As Jesus reminds us, "For where your treasure is, there your heart will be also" (Matthew 6:21). We all faithfully serve our gods. The question is, which god do you serve?

Providing emotional affirmation

Providing for the emotional needs of my wife and children should come as a natural overflow of my personal spiritual experience. The Apostle John declared in his first letter to the churches, "God is love. Whoever lives in love lives in God, and God in him" (1 John 4:16). Likewise, Paul told the Galatians that the "the fruit of the Spirit is love . . ." (Galatians 5:22). Note, that this love is a "fruit." I have never seen fruit sweat from toil. Fruit is the consequence of the tree being rooted in good, secure, nourishing soil. As you allow the roots of your personal devotional life go deep into God, you will naturally produce fruit after its kind: LOVE!

Practically, love takes on visible expression as it is made aware of needs in those under its care. We never neglect the things we treasure. This translates into some very practical actions.

1. Prayer: We pray for those for whom we have concern. We ask that God's protection and provision be given them in every circumstance. As Samuel declared to Saul ". . . far be it from me that I should sin against the LORD by failing to pray for you. And I will teach you the way that is good and right" (1 Samuel 12:23).

2. Teaching: We train those we love in ways that will enable them to grow spiritually on their own. Moses describes a wonderful model. He instructed Israel:

> These commandments that I give you today are to be upon your hearts. Impress them on your children. Talk about them when you sit at home and when you walk along the road, when you lie down and when you get up. Tie them as symbols on your hands and bind them on your foreheads. Write them on the door-frames of your houses and on your gates (Deuteronomy 6:6-9).

What is portrayed by his words is a life penetrated at every intersection with the presence of God. It is not something done out of habit or obligation. It is the natural outpouring of a heart that daily feasts upon God and His Word, whose presence is not occasional but constant.

It requires a man to see God as more than someone to be visited for an hour or so on Sunday mornings at our local house of worship. It's recognizing that God isn't dependent upon my worship (though He is pleased by it and desires it), but I desperately need to worship God regularly. It infers an awareness of His presence, everywhere, all the time, of His desire to commune with us in every aspect of our lives, in every moment of our days.

I love to take walks on summer evenings. Often, one or more of my children will accompany me. I have found it to be one of the best times to discuss spiritual things. They have many questions about the Bible and how to apply it to their lives. Their questions come naturally and honestly. I can't help but feel that this is the manner of instruction that God gave to Israel through Moses. "Let them see your devotion to Me at all times," He was saying. "Then they will know that I am not just a part of your life, but all of your life."

My children have had the opportunity to sit under my teaching as a pastor for years. But if you ask them, they will tell you that is not where they see God in my life. That happens at home.

3. Cherishing: We handle valuables tenderly. We set them up high, in places where they will be safe and appreciable to others. We patch them when they are broken, often shedding a tear of sadness, sorrow or regret.

As God increases our sense of the value our wives and children have in our lives, we begin to do the same. We highly esteem them, taking every occasion to speak well of them to others. When they are hurt, we are there to comfort and, if possible, aid their healing. We often feel their pain and sadness. When they are wounded, it is as if we ourselves had been wounded.

Listen to how Paul described his emotional concern for his "children" in the faith: "But we were gentle among you, like a mother caring for her little children . . . . For what is our hope, our joy, or the crown in which we will glory in the presence of our Lord Jesus when He comes? Is it not you?" (1 Thessalonians 2:7,19). He sounds like a proud father!

Men, we need to be a combination of tough and tender. Tough when it comes to protection from the things which can injure those we love; tender when it's time to care and comfort.

Providing for the financial needs of my family

We end where most of us would prefer to begin. That shouldn't surprise us. Most of us spend a good deal of our lives getting things backward. The allure to view your responsibilities in primarily financial terms is great. It is the dominant voice, the one that makes the most noise and therefore attracts our attention most often.

There is no other activity which is more revealing about our priorities than how we view and handle money. When we look to the Bible, we find that money is one of the more slippery issues with which we have to deal. Money's significance in our lives is far out of proportion to its real value. For many, it is a powerful stumbling block.

A major cause of divorce

The most commonly stated reason for marital failure is financial stress. Why? There is nothing more stressful to a wife than financial instability. How many fights and arguments have you and your wife had over money? I don't need to tell you that it is a serious problem, but few people have a clear understanding of how to handle money. Fewer still realize that the main reason people have money problems is not because of a shortage of funds; it is mainly due to mismanagement of the money they have.

Solomon declared as much: "Much food is in the tillage of the poor: but there is that is destroyed for want of judgment" (Proverbs 13:23, KJV). When we read this, our first conclusion is that poverty comes because of injustice done toward us. But it also refers to a lack of wise judgment in the management of our money.

For most of our married life, my wife and I had a very low income. It forced us to become very frugal. My wife still uses coupons to buy groceries. We never pay full retail for clothing and household items. If we want something, we comparison shop and wait for it to go on sale. We often have to ask ourselves if it is something we need or just want. Through our carefulness, we have been able to stretch dollars far beyond what many believe possible.

Recently, we hosted a tour of Israel through our church. One of the ladies who signed up to go did not have the money, but she believed that the Lord wanted her to go with us. She prayed and asked the Lord to provide. She began to do odd jobs, and as she received each paycheck, she would quickly put it into the bank before she had a chance to spend it. By the time the final payment was due, she had saved enough and more for the trip. What was most impacting to me as she shared her story was the lesson that she and her husband learned. "We have never been able to save money," she shared, "but now I know that we can if we put our minds to it."

Providing a stable standard of living is vitally important to your wife's sense of security and well being. Granted, there are times when God wants to teach both husband and wife to trust Him by cutting their income short. But generally speaking, His will is for stability and consistency.

If that isn't happening in your family, seek counsel from a Christian financial counselor. Maybe someone in your church is qualified to help you. Ask your pastor to recommend someone to whom you can speak.

I know this may be embarrassing. I have found that admitting financial problems is one of the hardest things for a man to do. We feel like we are failures. But change can only come through acknowledgement and confession. Don't allow your ego to hold you back from taking steps that can save your marriage.

Whose money is it?

We should not think of our money as being our own, to do with as we please. It is God's, given to us through His mercy and grace (1 Chronicles 29:14). It is to be used:

1. First, to honor God and further the Gospel through our tithes and offerings (Proverbs 3:9,10).

2. Second, to provide for the needs of (and to bless) our family.

3. Third, to relieve the sufferings and hardships of others (1 John 3:17).

God holds us accountable for the way we manage our money (Luke 16:10-12). If we are faithful with what He gives us, He will faithfully provide more. If we are unfaithful, he will withhold his blessing (Haggai 1:6).

Worse than an unbeliever?

There are two ways in which we can fail to provide financially for our families. The first is the most obvious. We read earlier Paul's instruction to Timothy, "If anyone does not provide for his relatives, and especially for his immediate family, he has denied the faith and is worse than an unbeliever" (1 Timothy 5:8). Financial provision is not something that should be done grudgingly, or only when we have an excess or an abundance. It even means giving when we have to go without ourselves.

I regret to say that I have known men who have been so self-centered they make sure all of their own needs and desires are met first, then they use what is left over to care for their families. It should be obvious to any truly Christian man that when it comes to the allocation of his resources he is to ensure that the needs of his wife and children are met first, then he is free to attend to his own needs.

A man is to be sacrificial in the way he provides for his family. When he isn't, it reveals a motive of greed. He is show-ing a covetous and idolatrous faith in the power of money, rather than the love and power of God (Colossians 3:5). Be-cause our God is a jealous God, He is very short with those who make money the focus of their affection. It is an evil heart that He will chasten. It is for this reason Paul warns, "For the love of money is a root of all kinds of evil. Some people, eager for money, have wandered from the faith and pierced them-selves with many griefs" (1 Timothy 6:10).

Through the years, I have seen many Christian men come to great prosperity. In most cases, it changes them. In the be-ginning, they were overwhelmed and humbled by the gracious increase God gave to their endeavors. Over time, an arrogance began to creep in—like Nebuchadnezzar of old who declared, "Is not this the great Babylon I have built as the royal residence, by my mighty power and for the glory of my majesty?" (Daniel 4:30). Just as God humbled Nebuchadnezzar, in time He humbled the men I've seen. In some cases, the results were tragic. Even after their fortunes were taken, they still were filled with its desire. Some lost more than their money; their wives and children went away as well. In the end they were "pierced . . .with many griefs."

The lessons we communicate

Recently, a well known professional athlete, responding to criticism about his behavior, declared that he wasn't a role model. The absurdity of his statement was not lost to many. He is a role model by virtue of his public persona. It is not something that he can control. Like it or not, millions of young people will imitate him simply because he is such a successful and recognizable public figure.

The same is true of husbands and fathers. Whether or not you realize it or accept it, you are a role model to your wife and children. It is a function of your position as the head of your home. They will imitate you, both in the good and the bad.

Why is this so? God has designed the home as a place of development for children. The mother and father both provide essential and yet differing functions. Children need both. When one or the other is missing, a central element necessary for proper training and development is missed, and the children suffer.

The role of the mother is to provide a "nest" for her brood, a place where they can feed and be nurtured. Moms give their children a sense of safety, security and emotional warmth. Even after we become adults, if our home was a normal one, we have warm feelings when we return. There is a comfortable safety about the place where we were raised. It has little to do with the building or the community. Rather, it is the result of a mother's care and nurturing.

The role of the father is to contribute to the development of the basic elements of personality. Confidence, independence, achievement orientation, self-discipline, morality and sex typing come primarily through the father's example. It happens quietly as our children watch us live out our lives before them. They learn by watching what and how we do what we do. They develop their own set of priorities by seeing what our priorities are.

If you want your children to be generous, be generous yourself. If you want them to be selfish and self-centered, think only about meeting your own needs. They will pick up quickly that it is every man for himself. I have found the most sobering and humbling part of being a husband and parent is that our wives and children reflect who we are far more than who we claim to be.

What is the message your life communicates to your wife and children about money? You can tell them that it is not the most important thing, but is that what your life says? If my conversation is always about money, if I am worried and stressed over not having enough or losing it, am I not saying that money is of greatest importance? If I am wasteful and indulgent, if I fail to honor God with my money, don't I communicate that money's purpose is to serve my needs first and foremost? We should follow the example of Paul as he gave his farewell message to the elders of the church of Ephesus: "In everything I did, I showed you that by this kind of hard work we must help the weak, remembering the words the Lord Jesus himself said: `It is more blessed to give than to receive'" (Acts 20:35).

When it comes to meeting the financial and material needs of your family, see your first goal as being an example of faith, generosity, service and sacrifice.

You can't buy love

The last thing I want to say on this topic is that you can't replace love with money. It is so cliche' to state this, that I didn't even want to. But I suspect that some of you are doing just this without realizing it.

If you are strapped financially, this probably doesn't apply to you. It is actually the direct opposite of what we have discussed previously.

Your wife and children need you more than they need your money. They need to know how you think, what your feelings are, that you love them more than any other thing in your life.

When they call you at work, you need to take time to listen to them. You need to make time in your schedule for them; to take vacations together; to sit and talk leisurely about the issues, concerns, pleasures and problems of their lives. They have thousands of questions that only you can answer; a thousand things to say that only you can hear.

They need your money, but they also need your time and your energy. If you give them one or two but neglect the other, eventually it will take its toll. Invest in your family and you will reap rewards beyond your highest expectations. Neglect them, and you will grow old with sorrow and regret.

10

Women Who Will Not Follow!

My son, do not forget my teaching, but keep my commands in your heart, for they will prolong your life many years and bring you prosperity. Let love and faithfulness never leave you; bind them around your neck, write them on the tablet of your heart. Then you will win favor and a good name in the sight of God and man. Trust in the LORD with all your heart and lean not on your own understanding; in all your ways acknowledge him, and he will make your paths straight. Do not be wise in your own eyes; fear the LORD and shun evil. This will bring health to your body and nourishment to your bones (Proverbs 3: 1-8).

There is another side to the leadership issue that is not faced as openly as male abdication. It is the increasing unwillingness of women to submit to their husbands' leadership.

Encouraged by modern feminism, increasing numbers of women believe they will be happiest if they can maintain as much independence from their husbands as possible. To a large degree, they have bought into the message of the 1970s, "Woman, you don't need a man." This belief was well characterized by a joke that traveled among "consciousness raising" groups of the decade. It went like this, "A woman without a man is like a fish without a bicycle."

The initial effects of this "new thinking" were almost immediately disastrous. In 1967, the number of men who deserted their families far outweighed women who did the same. For every 500 men who left, there was only one woman. By 1977, the pendulum had swung dramatically in the other direction. In that year, two women deserted their families for every man who did so.

Today, many of those women are realizing they made a mistake. Kay Ebling, writing in an editorial for Newsweek magazine summed it up pretty well:

> Today I see feminism as the Great Experiment That Failed, and women in my generation, its perpetrators, are the casualties. Many of us, myself included, are saddled with raising children alone. The resulting poverty makes us experts in cornmeal recipes and ways to find free recreation on weekends. At the same time, single men from our generation amass fortunes in CDs and real-estate ventures so they can breeze off on ski weekends. Feminism freed men, not women. Now men are spared the nuisance of a wife and family to support. After childbirth, if his wife's waist doesn't return to 20 inches, the husband can go out and get a more petite woman. It's far more difficult for the wife, now tied down with a baby, to find a new man . . . .
>
> What's worse, we asked for it. Many women decided: you don't need a family structure to raise your children. We packed them off to day-care centers where they could get their nurturing from professionals. Then we put on our suits and ties, packed our briefcases and took off on this Great Experiment, convinced that there was no difference between ourselves and the guys in the other offices.
>
> How wrong we were . . . . The reality of feminism is a lot of frenzied and overworked women dropping kids off at day-care centers.[23]

This isn't the way the media reports it, but those who have followed this path know that Ms. Ebling's comments reflect reality.

What were these women running from, anyway? I am convinced that feminism would never have occurred if men had been the kind of leaders God had intended in the home. If men had loved and cherished their wives as Christ does His church, if they had been willing to protect, provide and sacrifice as He has commanded, women would have never even thought of breaking out from under their husbands' headship.

Having said that, feminism in all its modifications and variant forms was and is still a bad idea. The proof is in the pudding. The consequences are evident, and they don't lie.

These unfortunate women were trying to go against a law of the universe as inviolable as gravity. It is impossible to defy gravity. We can climb in a plane and fly over the face of the earth, but eventually you have to land. You can't sustain this defiance of gravity forever. Sooner or later the law of gravity wins out.

So also with God's laws. You can rebel against them and live without regard to His ways. For a while you will feel free, independent, liberated. But before long, the reality of life overtakes even the most committed. Then you are faced with the consequences of your choices—for the rest of your life! The toll in lost time, lost relationships and lost opportunities is often devastating.

Reversing the trend

As with any diagnosis of a problem, we must also recommend a cure. In this case, it is merely a matter of going back to the principles which God outlined from the beginning. Men need to lead as God has commanded them to; and women need to follow.

The "fly in the ointment" is our sin nature. We find ourselves often unwilling to submit to God's way. Fear and self-will often lead us to rebel against all kinds of authority. We all do it with great regularity. Every man is guilty of disobeying God. Every woman is guilty of disobeying her husband. All children rebel against their parents.

As with most sin, we can see it clearly in others, but we have a hard time recognizing it in ourselves. When someone rebels against us, we are quick to see how wrong it is. When we rebel against others, we are quick to rationalize why it is right, even necessary.

The Bible clearly teaches that people are the happiest when their lives are patterned in accordance with the way God has created them — in submission to God's ways and will. Because our natural "bent" is to drift away or rebel against God's way, we often find ourselves in need of repentance. Unfortunately, many of us are a little fuzzy on what repentance actually looks like. Probably the best definition of repentance I have ever read was given by William Barclay. Here's how he explained it:

> What does repentance mean? The word originally meant an afterthought. Often a second thought shows that the first thought was wrong; and so the word came to mean a change of mind. But, if a man is honest, a change of mind demands a change of action. Repentance must involve both change of mind and change of action. A man may change his mind and come to see that his actions were wrong, but be so much in love with his old ways that he will not change them. A man may change his ways but his mind remains the same, changing only because of fear or prudence. True repentance involved a change of mind and a change of action.[24]

If marriages and families are ever going to reach their fullest potential, there must be a willingness for both husband and wife to accept the way God has ordained for them to function—a change of mind and action.

The path of repentance

Men must repent of past neglect and insensitivity and begin showing leadership—spiritually, emotionally and physically. Women must repent of past bitterness and hostility and begin to honor and encourage their husband's role as the leaders of their homes. They need to model submission to authority before their children so their children will likewise respect authority.

How many times has a mother become frustrated by her children's disobedience, yet failed to see that she frequently disregards her husband's will and desires? How often has a man been hurt or angered at a wife who is unloving or untrusting of his leadership, yet he is unwilling to trust God in even the smallest things? Respect for our authority comes from our modeling respect for those who are in authority over us. If we want others to respect us in our positions of leadership, we must begin by showing respect for those who are in authority over us.

In the early years of my pastorate, I harbored a bitterness toward the man whom God had placed in authority over me. This bitterness manifested itself in unkind and critical comments about him to others. I knew it was sin, but I was high-minded. As is true with most judgmental people, I thought I was justified in what I was doing. "I am right and he is wrong," was my attitude. The belief that I was right seemed ample justification.

Then God began to show me the cause and effect relationship of my behavior. I found that many in my church were highly critical of me. In fact, they began to criticize me in exactly the same ways I was criticizing the one over me. One day, as I was complaining to the Lord about these unkind and ungrateful people, the Lord opened my eyes to my sin. Literally, I was "reaping what I had sown." I was being "judged by the same judgment whereby I had judged others." I had forgotten that "mercy will be shown to those who show mercy," and criticism to those who are critical.

So how did I deal with my sin? First, I confessed it to God, not that God needed to know. God was the one who made me aware of my sin in the first place. But I needed to acknowledge the wrongness of my attitude and consequent behavior. Then I made an appointment with my pastor and confessed my sin to him, asking his forgiveness.

What followed was wonderful. My pastor graciously forgave my arrogance, and joyously, our fellowship was restored. I also spent some time confessing my sin to others with whom I had "shared" my complaints.

Since that time, those who were critical of me have either left the church or repented to me personally. The atmosphere of the church went from being critical to being loving and supportive. My congregation is so gracious to my wife and me that it is sometimes embarrassing.

If you are a husband who has neglected your role as the spiritual leader in your home, if you have not been seeking God for the needs of your family, you need to repent to God, and then to your family, asking their forgiveness.

If you are a wife who has been unwilling to trust your husband, failing to show him respect as the head of your home, you need to likewise repent to God and your husband.

As you humble yourselves before one another in this manner, you will begin to lay a spiritual foundation upon which your family can be rebuilt. You will be inviting Christ to become the leader of your home and your lives. His presence will make a profound difference.

Two leadership styles

Leadership usually comes in one of two forms. One is called Authoritative Leadership. This is preferred and is rare. The other is called Authoritarian Leadership. Authoritarian leadership is far more common and is the style we think of when we talk about leadership.

For many, all leadership is seen as being authoritarian. To be authoritarian means "the exercise of authority without external restraint." When people behave in this way, they act arbitrarily, autocratically, despotically, tyrannically. They view leadership authority as a license to do whatever they please. They act independent of others, except when they encounter someone who has more power. Then they submit, but only temporarily. Their goal is to gain more power, usually at the expense of others.

This is not the authority principle the Bible teaches. What the Bible teaches is Authoritative Leadership. The word authoritative means, "worthy of acceptance because of its accuracy." Synonyms for this kind of leadership are "authentic, credible, faithful, trustworthy." Authoritative leaders begin by seeing that one's authority does not originate from oneself, rather, it is delegated to them by God. Such leaders realize that God will hold them accountable for the manner in which they exercise that authority. Authority has been given them for the purpose of serving others, and in the context of the family, it is service toward a wife and children.

James makes reference to this regarding teachers in the church: "Not many of you should presume to be teachers, my brothers, because you know that we who teach will be judged more strictly" (James 3:1). James recognized that the position of "teacher" in the church carries great authority with it. A teacher can lead a group of people in both holy and unholy directions. Therefore, he warns the teachers, "you will be judged" by a stricter measurement. This involves yet another principle: "For unto whomsoever much is given, of him shall be much required: and to whom men have committed much, of him they will ask the more" (Luke 12:48).

I believe it was Lord Ashton who first stated, "Power corrupts, and absolute power corrupts absolutely." God, recognizing this human weakness, seeks to prevent the abuse of power by a system of accountability. For the man of God, His Word regularly reminds us that God sees and will judge us according to the manner in which we exercise our authority. It is given to serve, nurture and bless. If we use it for selfish reasons, He will punish us. We must learn to lead tenderly.

> But we were gentle among you, like a mother caring for her little children (1 Thessalonians 2:7).

A word about harshness

I have spoken extensively about the differences that exist between men and women. There is yet one more dimension to this issue I must explain. It applies to the way we communicate with one another. Hopefully, what I have to say will enable you to be more sensitive to one another.

Men tend to be harsh, and women tend to be cruel. Before you react, read on and let me explain.

A man's world is, by its very nature, more harsh than a woman's. When men play, they are far more physical than women. Men like contact sports. Even when we play noncontact sports, like basketball or baseball, we end up slamming our bodies against the floor, the ground, one another. Afterward, we get up and hug or pat one another on the back. No hard feelings as long as it falls within the rules of the game, often loosely interpreted.

When we joke, we poke fun at one another in ways that would drive most women to tears. We give each other nicknames that would humiliate the average woman. Much of what men do, they do to win. We strive to triumph. In contrast, it is women who say things like, "It's just a game." They put as much importance on the process as they do the results.

In conversation, a man wants to know what the point or objective is so he can provide answers and solutions. If his wife begins a conversation with a problem, he attacks like an interrogator: "Just the facts, ma'am!" His objective is to "solve the problem." I can't even begin to count the number of times my wife has become frustrated with me over this. She will stop me and say, "I don't want you to give me answers. I know what the Bible says. I know that everything I am feeling isn't right. But I just want someone to talk to; someone who will listen to me!"

Frankly, for most men, this is a stretch. Nevertheless, if men are ever going to learn how to talk to women, we need to understand that our "Mr. Fix-it" approach is too harsh and insensitive for most women. Being listened to, being understood, is critical to a woman's emotional needs. A woman values most the man who will allow her the space to express her feelings through words. Men find emotional release through action. Women find it through words.

To some degree, this is due to our physical differences, but it also involves our personality differences. It is far more common for men to be blunt, direct and harsh in our words with one another than it is for women. It's as if words hold less meaning for men than they do for women. Men can forget a verbal offense far more quickly than most women, especially if it is followed by an apology. Women tend to have elephantine memories. They cling to words and statements made in anger and haste as if they were the Decalogue itself.

Men, when you are angry with your wives, guard your words very carefully. Words spoken in haste toward women and children can crush their spirits. Remember that childhood rhyme, "Sticks and stones may break my bones, but words will never hurt me"? The truth is words can kill.

Remember the words of James:

> Likewise the tongue is a small part of the body, but it makes great boasts. Consider what a great forest is set on fire by a small spark. The tongue also is a fire, a world of evil among the parts of the body. It corrupts the whole person,

sets the whole course of his life on fire, and is itself set on fire
by hell. All kinds of animals, birds, reptiles and creatures of
the sea are being tamed and have been tamed by man, but no
man can tame the tongue. It is a restless evil, full of deadly
poison. With the tongue we praise our Lord and Father, and
with it we curse men, who have been made in God's likeness. Out of the same mouth come praise and cursing. My
brothers, this should not be (James 3:5-10).

Men, learn to tame your tongues. Use them as tools to build,
not weapons to defend or attack.

Pecking hens

Ladies, I pray that you will forgive me for making an un-
flattering comparison. Have you ever raised chickens? When
you first pick them up at the feed store, they are so-o-o cute—
soft, yellow, round and fluffy all over. But before long their
true nature begins to come out.

That's because life in the chicken yard is every bird for himself. As long as there is food enough and space enough, things
go OK. Then one day, something different happens. It only
takes a small drop of blood on one of the chickens and the scene
turns grisly.

As soon as one chicken senses that spot of blood, she begins to peck at it. Quickly, she is joined by others. They peck
and peck and peck. Before you know it, the victim lies dead
on the ground.

The above describes a man's view of women when they
come under their criticism. The term they use to describe your
actions is "hen-pecked." To call a man hen-pecked threatens
his very identity as a man.

The most wounding thing a woman can do to a man is to
regularly point out his faults and failings. Why, you ask? Because most men derive their sense of worth as a man by their
ability to make you happy. There is nothing more crushing to
his self-concept than his inability to make you happy. You can't
handle his harshness and insensitivity? He can't handle your
criticism!

I know some of you are reading this and saying to your-self, "Well if he would just change then I would stop criticizing him."

There are basically three errors in your thinking.

1. Many women use their husbands as a stress release. They will ventilate anger and frustration upon their husbands, even when their husband isn't the cause. Stress from the job or from raising children is dumped upon their husbands because they know they couldn't express these same emotions to their bosses or friends and still have a job and friends. You may reason that he has it easier than you and is therefore somehow responsible for your conflicts. Or you may think he can handle it and there-fore it shouldn't matter. To you it may be "just blowing off some steam." To him, it is crushing and demoralizing.

2. Many women complain out of habit. They don't even hear themselves doing it.

3. Most women mistakenly think they can change their husbands through pointing out their faults and failings to them. Let me clarify that one for you: You can't!

I'm not saying that it is impossible for him to change or that he will never change. I'm just pointing out that you are not going to be the one who does it. In fact, no human can change another, truly. Only God can. God changes hearts, not just outward actions.

In the meantime, your words may be slowly killing any desire he may have to change or to please you. He may not be able to hear what God is saying to him because you are drown-ing out the "still, small voice" of God.

For years, my wife complained about my fast driving. Ev-ery time she did, it only offended me. I interpreted her com-plaints as criticism of me as a person. Every time she would get upset, I felt rejected. It was as if she was saying that I was incompetent.

Eventually, I began to modify my driving, but not because of her complaints. It started when God began to convict me of being a law breaker, someone who was only thinking of his own interests and not others. I began to think about how ter-rible it would be if I were to injure or kill someone. I started thinking about the example I was setting for my kids and what kind of drivers they would become.

To tell you the truth, it took me longer to change because of my wife's criticism than if I had to deal with God alone. He was much more effective in getting my attention. He used a series of traffic citations, which eventually resulted in the cancellation of my insurance. Now that got my attention.

What is a man's response to a critical wife? He becomes bitter. Once that happens, he usually withdraws into a place of safety. He may simply sit in the corner and watch TV or read the paper. He may find things to take him out of the home such as sports, hobbies or friends. For him it is a natural response to pain. Your criticism causes deep pain, and he will do whatever he needs to do to avoid it.

Ladies, your husband wants to be your hero. Don't only tell him what he is doing wrong. Tell him the things he does right. And when something comes up that bothers you, don't focus on the negative. Instruct him on the positive. Tell him what it is that you would like him to do, rather than complaining about what he has done wrong.

For example, if you need help with the housework, don't tell him how lazy or selfish he is. Never compare him to somebody else's husband, rather share with him your burden. Tell him how much you would appreciate it if he could help you out. He probably won't begin to take the initiative right away, but each time he sees you doing housework, in his mind he'll be thinking about what you shared with him. God will coax and challenge him. It may take a while for him to catch on. So pray for him, and ask the Lord to put it on his heart to lend a hand.

When you approach your issues in this way, you allow him room to change. In the end, his desire to be your hero, to please you by doing those things that you ask him to, will overcome all his bad habits.

Trust me, I know what I am talking about. I have been there.

What is it that you are really looking for from your husband?

The other day, I was attending one of my son's basketball games. Halfway through, the mother of one of the other players on my son's team, who also attends my church, sat beside me and began to talk. I can't remember how we got on the subject of marriage, but she began to share with me the wonderful way in which God had been working in hers. Let me paraphrase her comments.

> Soon after we were married, I began to get really angry at my husband. He's an avid golfer. He was always on the phone to his buddies planning golf outings. He would put such effort and preparation into these golf times. He'd call and schedule tee times, sometimes having to coordinate several different schedules with available times at the course. They would plan lunch and various other get-togethers, all revolving around golf.
>
> I found that this made me really angry, but I couldn't figure out why. My rational mind said it was silly for me to feel this way, but inside I was raging. So, I began to pray about my feelings. Then it hit me. I was jealous. He never put that much effort into spending time with me. If we went out to dinner, it was my idea. Often I would have to make all the arrangements. He rarely acted like he was excited about it; at least the way he was about golf. I knew he had it in him to be that excited because I had seen it in his interest in golf. I wanted him to be that way with me.

What really blessed me is what she did next. She sat her husband down and told him what she had come to realize. She did it without condemning or yelling. She apologized for the irrationality of her anger in the past. Then she explained to him what it was that she wanted from him: to be at least as devoted to her as he was to golf.

In so doing, she had put her issue into terms he could easily understand. After she finished, he apologized for not being more sensitive and promised from that day forward it would be different. She told me that he kept his word.

She said, "I wish I could share with every woman I know how lucky I am."

11

Romance In Marriage

How beautiful you are, my darling! Oh, how beautiful! Your
eyes behind your veil are doves. Your hair is like a flock of
goats descending from Mount Gilead. Your teeth are like a
flock of sheep just shorn, coming up from the washing. Each
has its twin; not one of them is alone. Your lips are like a
scarlet ribbon; your mouth is lovely. Your temples behind
your veil are like the halves of a pomegranate. Your neck is
like the tower of David, built with elegance; on it hang a thousand shields, all of them shields of warriors. Your two breasts
are like two fawns, like twin fawns of a gazelle that browse
among the lilies. Until the day breaks and the shadows flee,
I will go to the mountain of myrrh and to the hill of incense.
All beautiful you are, my darling; there is no flaw in you.
Come with me from Lebanon, my bride, come with me from
Lebanon. Descend from the crest of Amana, from the top of
Senir, the summit of Hermon, from the lions' dens and the
mountain haunts of the leopards. You have stolen my heart,
my sister, my bride; you have stolen my heart with one glance
of your eyes, with one jewel of your necklace. How delight-
ful is your love, my sister, my bride! How much more pleasing is your love than wine, and the fragrance of your per-
fume than any spice! Your lips drop sweetness as the honey-
comb, my bride; milk and honey are under your tongue. The
fragrance of your garments is like that of Lebanon. You are a
garden locked up, my sister, my bride; you are a spring en-
closed, a sealed fountain. Your plants are an orchard of pome-
granates with choice fruits, with henna and nard, nard and
saffron, calamus and cinnamon, with every kind of incense
tree, with myrrh and aloes and all the finest spices. You are a
garden fountain, a well of flowing water streaming down
from Lebanon. Awake, north wind, and come, south wind!
Blow on my garden, that its fragrance may spread abroad.
Let my lover come into his garden and taste its choice fruits
(Song of Songs 4:1-16)

I don't know how they got my name, but there it was; an envelope from Playboy Magazine. I opened it and read the following:

> Because of your proven good taste, we are inviting you to represent "The Sophisticated Male of The Nineties" and help PLAYBOY Magazine construct "The Perfect Woman."
> You read it right! From the many intelligent men in and around your state, we have selected YOU for our 1994 Perfect Woman Poll. PLAYBOY wants your insights, ideas and comments on exactly what your "perfect woman" would look like and how she would act . . . .
> No doubt you have visualized "her," even seen her in your dreams.
> You might have hoped for years to walk past her on the street. Ride with her in an elevator. Or, sit next to her in a meeting, a train or a plane. (Maybe, just maybe, you are one of the lucky ones who have actually found her!)
> At the very least, we know, as a full-blooded male, you probably have put her together, this "Perfect Woman." Piece by piece. Trait by trait—in your mind's eye!

Are these guys serious? What followed was a two-page questionnaire covering all kinds of topics like, "I believe the perfect woman's measurements would be . . . ." I don't even know what my wife's measurements are!

They asked for specific answers to everything you could imagine regarding a person: beauty, body parts, brains, fashion, lifestyle, workstyle, sexual attitudes. To be honest, they asked about things that I bet few men have ever taken the time to think about.

Which tells me something about this survey. It had to have been written by a woman. This is the kind of minutiae that women think about, not men. No man would refer to his contemporaries as a "full-blooded male," nor would he spend the time trying to analyze what the perfect woman looks like. A man's initial decision as to whether he finds a woman attractive is completed within the first 15-20 seconds of meeting her. Whether the level of attraction goes up or down from there is based upon a man's perception of the woman's personality, not her bust size!

Hyper-romantics

Where else in the world do you get this kind of garbage in the mail? Only in America. Most places would consider it bad taste and nobody else's business. Most cultures are not nearly as hyped-up about sex as ours is.

I doubt few would argue with me when I say we live in a hyper-romanticized culture. If you don't think so, just turn on your radio and listen to the lyrics of the songs. Turn on your TV and see what's playing. Ninety percent of programming deals with love and romance. Walk through your local bookstore, video store, grocery check-out stand. What you will find is an overwhelming obsession with romance, love and sexuality. There is no other topic which is more talked about, thought about, sung about, written about, even dreamed about—than true love and romance!

Consider some of our favorite phrases—

"Love is blind."

"All mankind loves a lover."

"Love means never having to say you're sorry."

"Tis better to have loved and lost, than to have never

loved at all."

"How do I love thee? Let me count the ways."

Bill Hybels summarized it as well as it could be:

Love. It makes the world go round, conquers all and warps the mind. We are star-crossed by it, swept away by it, fall into it. It can't be bought, but some have paid dearly for it. All's fair in it. Wars have been fought for it and kingdoms renounced for it. It's better than wine, sweeter than candy and more glorious than a summer's day. And anyone will tell you it's better to have done it and lost than never to have done it at all.[25]

Yet, for all our focus, fascination and fantasy over love and romance, how many of us ever really come to understand it as

God intended? What do we really know about romance?

Unfailing love

Why is it that we are so obsessed with love and romance? Scripture gives a simple and direct answer: "What a man desires is unfailing love" (Proverbs 19:22). Unfortunately, most of us soon discover that romance is often not the same as unfailing love.

C. S. Lewis, in his classic book, The Four Loves, explained the basic problem we encounter with romance in terms of what he called Venus:

> Venus will sometimes slip back into mere sexuality. What's ten times worse, that desire for the beloved herself, for total unity may take on a morbid form. It may come to be a sort of imperialism, a desire for absorbing rather than being absorbed, possessing without being possessed, making the beloved, every thought, wish, interest, a reflection of oneself. And since the beloved may have exactly the same programming, success which should be infamous if achieved, should not be very probable.[26]

In other words, the natural selfish bent of our human nature, unrestrained by a strong conscience and/or the Holy Spirit, will always deteriorate into sensuality and conquest. The beloved becomes an object to be possessed and absorbed, rather than cherished and nourished.

A problem of definition

Because of this problem, it has become necessary to clearly define what we mean when we say to someone, "I love you." We English speakers are more limited in communicating precisely what we mean than those who speak some other languages. The Greeks, for example, have four different terms to define the exact character and kind of love to which they are referring. They have a word for family love (*storge*), romantic love (*eros*), brotherly love (*philia*), and altruistic love (*agape*).

In contrast, when we say "I love you," one has to determine the nature of that love by the context in which it is given. If a husband says it to his wife, it means one thing. If the same man says it to a son or daughter, it should mean something very different. If he says it to a parent or a friend, it means still something different again.

What this tells us is that we have to be more thoughtful about how we express our various feelings of love and the limits we place around its expression. We also must recognize that others may place a far different meaning on our words of love, based instead upon what they have experienced with us than what we say. If a man tells his wife that he loves her and that is always followed by an effort to persuade her to engage in sex, then every time he tells her he loves her, she will hear him saying, "I want sex," which may or may not be the case.

If we look in our dictionaries, we find that even the word romance once meant something different than it does to us today. To our forefathers, it meant something that was chivalrous; ideal; the highest personification of love, sacrifice and duty. Later it came to mean something that was fanciful and unrealistic.

Today, romance is used almost exclusively in reference to sexual behavior. For many, romantic behavior is anything that will culminate in a sexual encounter.

Valentine's day

As I write this, Valentine's Day is less than a week away. I was reminded of an incident that happened to me last year at this time that I believe illustrates this problem of communication.

It was once very easy for me to shop for a Valentine's Day gift for my wife. She has a specific brand of chocolates that she loves. My job was to make sure I purchased her an ample supply each year.

Lately, she has become concerned about gaining weight and eating more nutritionally (despite the fact that she hasn't gained a pound in ten years). She declared, "Don't buy me any chocolate. Too many fat grams." This left me perplexed. What was I going to get her? Everything I could afford she already has. And the things I can't afford, she'd return.

Finally, sensing my dilemma, she had pity and told me that

she would like a pair of silk pajamas.   I was off like a shot to the mall, accompanied by my twelve-year-old son. (I rely upon him for all final decisions when it comes to buying clothing for my wife. He is rarely right, but he has strong opinions, which aids me in making a decision.)

As we entered a national chain store, known for its specialization in feminine undergarments, I quickly began to feel uncomfortable. There were dozens of other men being helped by saleswomen. They were pawing through racks of women's undergarments that were so scant they hardly qualified to be called "garments."

Eventually, one of the helpful saleswomen, seeing my obvious bewilderment as a "stranger in a strange land," offered her assistance. When I told her that I was shopping for women's pajamas, she began showing me the same stuff that all the other guys were looking at. At that point, I explained to her that I was shopping for something to please my wife, not me. I told her that I couldn't imagine this stuff was in the least bit comfortable. The poor woman looked puzzled for a moment. She was not in the least impressed by the practicality of my purchase. I'm sure she questioned if there was a romantic bone in my body. I doubt that she realizes that "teddies" have little to do with romance, at least as God intended it.

Spirituality vs. romance

The era of the sexual revolution gave rise to certain assumptions, most which have been accepted without question or dispute, regarding religion and sex. Like east and west, it is suggested that the two can never meet. It is believed by large sectors of our society that people of faith have deep and sometimes disturbing, inhibitions regarding sexual intimacy, that we are up-tight about romance and live lives of restraint and simmering frustration.

That is why it came as such a shock when Redbook Magazine tallied the results of their nationwide survey of 18,349 female readers. They asked women to respond to hundreds of questions, indicating their views, feelings and beliefs regarding family, love, marriage, romance and sex. In no way did they anticipate the results they got.

They found that the more liberal and non-religious a woman was, the greater her level of dissatisfaction with romance and marriage, at every stage of her life. In contrast, conservative, religious women, with stricter views toward premarital and extramarital sex, stated higher degrees of satisfaction with their marriages, sex and romance. They also experience half as many divorces.[27]

Incorrect assumptions

One of the assumptions many people have about God and the Bible is that they are down on romance. If such people ever actually read the Bible, it would become immediately clear how incorrect this is. The Bible is full of stories that are very romantic. Adam and Eve, Abraham and Sarah, Isaac and Rebekkah, Jacob and Rachel—all are tales of true romance. The Song of Solomon is an expressly sensuous statement of love. Even when one views it as an allegory of God's love for Israel or the church, it gives God's love a dimension of passion that is exciting.

The Bible does not condemn romance. It presents it as a part and fact of normal life. To treat it any other way would be abnormal. What it does do is warn against illicit sensuality, especially when it is expressed outside the commitment of marriage.

A second incorrect assumption is that the Bible does not address or recognize the sexual side of our being. Again, the opposite is the case.

The Bible addresses the issue frequently and in detail, with the intent of bringing our sexuality under control so that it might serve us, rather than dominate and control us. Both sex and romance find their greatest fulfillment within the context of a committed and loving relationship, a relationship limited to one man and one woman, for life. God wants us to understand that the ultimate fulfillment and happiness to be found in a human relationship is found in the monogamous union of one man and one woman, for the totality of their lives.

Lastly, some have mistakenly concluded that the Bible is

against sex. Again, that is not at all what the Bible says. In
fact, it tells us just the opposite. In Proverbs, Solomon exhorts
men to:

> Let your fountain—of human life—be blessed [with the
> rewards of fidelity], and rejoice with the wife of your youth.
> Let her be as the loving hind and pleasant doe [tender, gentle,
> attractive]; and always be transported with delight in her love
> (Proverbs 5:18,19, Amplified).

Paul also gave the command that husbands and wives
should be careful not to withhold sexual intimacy with one
another, lest it lead to adultery.

> The husband should fulfill his marital duty to his wife,
> and likewise the wife to her husband. The wife's body does
> not belong to her alone but also to her husband. In the same
> way, the husband's body does not belong to him alone but
> also to his wife. Do not deprive each other except by mutual
> consent and for a time, so that you may devote yourselves to
> prayer. Then come together again so that Satan will not tempt
> you because of your lack of self-control (1 Corinthians 7:3-5).

It is unfaithfulness and adultery which God condemns. As the
writer of Hebrews instructs, "Marriage should be honored by
all, and the marriage bed kept pure, for God will judge the adul-
terer and all the sexually immoral (Hebrews 13:4).

Differing objectives

Men and women approach the issues of love, sex and romance from very different perspectives. They have very different needs, and therefore engage in sexual intimacy for very
different reasons. Each will evaluate the results of sexual intimacy based upon their own set of criteria. This, in itself, explains why sexual intimacy can oftentimes become so complex,
frustrating and even painful for couples.

Dr. Willard F. Harley, in his book, *His Needs, Her Needs*, states
that his counseling experience has enabled him to identify five
basic needs men expect their wives to fulfill, and five needs
women expect their husbands to meet.

The man's five most basic needs in marriage are:

1. Sexual fulfillment
2. Recreational companionship
3. An attractive spouse
4. Domestic support
5. Admiration

The woman's five most basic needs in marriage are:

1. Affection
2. Conversation
3. Honesty and openness
4. Financial support
5. Family commitment[28]

As you read over these ten needs, you can begin to see how they can both complement one another and also cause conflict. Sexual fulfillment, the #1 need on the man's list, doesn't even appear on the woman's. Her #1 need is for affection. (For men, affection is not the same as sex.) A man wants sex, and the woman wants affection. In most relationships, this translates into a trade off. The woman gives sex to get affection. The man shows affection to get sex.

Putting it in such graphic terms may make some of you feel uncomfortable, but we must come to grips with the fact that we are sexual beings. Jesus told His disciples that to be freed from the need and desire for marital sex is resultant only as a gift of God (Matthew 19:11,12). The normal human desire is to share sexual intimacy with another.

Yet again, it is the bargaining aspect of many relationships that often leads to conflict over sex. Sex is such a fragile part of our being that it must always be handled with the utmost care. There is never a moment when a man and woman are more vulnerable to one another than when they have opened their bodies to one another in sexual intercourse.

Female sexual response

When a woman yields her body to her husband, it is a statement of trust and submission. In a sense, she has willfully surrendered herself to him. She is expressing her confidence in his honesty, openness and commitment to her alone. For the most part, she is not looking for fireworks or excitement, rather, her desire is for tenderness and affection. How elegantly this is portrayed in the story of Ruth and Boaz. As she comes to Boaz late at night, laying down at his feet, she calls to him, "I am your servant Ruth. Spread the corner of your garment over me, since you are a kinsman-redeemer"(Ruth 3:9). It was her great respect and admiration, created through his generosity, protection and care toward her in her time of need, that caused her heart to open and embrace him in love.

The ancient rabbis described a woman as a fragile rose that must be allowed to open her petals slowly and at her own pace. She must be allowed to give herself freely. She does this only as the other needs in her life are met through her husband—her need for commitment, financial support, honesty and openness, and caring communication (i.e., listening to her). For most women, seduction must begin at the beginning of the day. For still others, it must begin at the beginning of the week. Passion is something that rises perilously and slowly until its culmination in intercourse.

Male sexual response

In contrast to women, men are pretty uncomplicated when it comes to sexual response. This, more than anything else, explains why men find women so confusing. Most men are aroused rather quickly, and subside even more quickly. The act itself is not as intense as it is for women nor as significant emotionally.

That is not to say that sex is a purely mechanical act on the part of a man. It plays a vital role in their sense of emotional well being.

Men are attracted to women who admire and support them.

When a woman lovingly surrenders her body in the sexual act to the man, it is the ultimate expression to him of admiration and support. Note that I said "lovingly surrenders." I make this distinction because I am well aware that many times women will "submit" to sexual relationship with their husbands, but not out of admiration and support. A sense of duty, responsibility, obligation often are the reasons. Sometimes a woman will yield just to keep her husband from bugging her.

I am not suggesting that couples should only engage in intercourse when both have reached an optimum desire. This would make intercourse far too rare in 99 percent of marriages. There will be times when a man or woman will consent to sex when they aren't completely in the mood. They do it because they want to respond to the need in their spouse, even though the desire in themselves is not that strong.

But it should be kept in mind that intercourse is not supposed to be a one-sided affair. If the only thing derived from it is sexual release, your spouse will quickly become dissatisfied with that aspect of your relationship. A sincere interest, even a playfulness, can and should be a regular part of your intimacy together.

When a woman withholds sex from her husband, it is crushing to his ego and identity. The same is true if she criticizes his performance. I often characterize men as being like eggs. They have a hard exterior. But if you drop them, they run out all over and make a big mess.

Don't assume that because a man can be rough and rugged, or he pretends that he is not hurt easily, that this is the way it is. A man depends upon your affirmation to give him the strength to face life's battles. When you believe in him, he believes in himself. When you don't, self-doubt cripples him.

Ladies, if you are struggling with this area of your relationship, then let your needs and feelings be known to your husband. Share with him what you would like to derive from sex in your marriage. Ask him what is pleasing to him.

Sex is not as straightforward as many people assume. At first, we are all rank amateurs. Our expectations are high, and our patience is low. The wonderful thing about it is that it has the potential to get better and better with time and practice. That depends, though, on learning from our mistakes. Couples need to communicate. They need to come to mutual agreement over what is comfortable and acceptable. It is never right to force or pressure your partner to engage in anything that he or she feels uncomfortable about or violates God's standards of righteousness.

Sexual intimacy is intended by God to be one of the richest and most fulfilling aspects of your life together as husband and wife. If we liken it to a flower, then commitment is the root and companionship is the stem. It is nurtured by sacrifice and service. Sexual intimacy is the blossom. Unfortunately in today's world, most people want only the blossom. They rush to pluck it off and savor its fragrance. Soon it withers and dies.

Is it any wonder that so many marriages fail so often?

12

Adultery -
The Marriage Killer

For the prostitute reduces you to a loaf of bread, and the adulteress preys upon your very life. Can a man scoop fire into his lap without his clothes being burned? Can a man walk on hot coals without his feet being scorched? So is he who sleeps with another man's wife; no one who touches her will go unpunished. Men do not despise a thief if he steals to satisfy his hunger when he is starving. Yet if he is caught, he must pay sevenfold, though it costs him all the wealth of his house. But a man who commits adultery lacks judgment; whoever does so destroys himself. Blows and disgrace are his lot, and his shame will never be wiped away; for jealousy arouses a husband's fury, and he will show no mercy when he takes revenge. He will not accept any compensation; he will refuse the bribe, however great it is (Proverbs 6: 26-35).

In the twenty-plus years I have been pastoring, I have had the honor of sharing in what I hope will be a once-in-a-life time experience with hundreds of couples. They have stood before me, their family and friends, publicly vowing to God and man that they will love, cherish, respect, to have and to hold, to keep themselves solely to their beloved, 'til death do them part, "so help me God."

I have no question at that moment they mean every word they are saying. To be certain, I remind them, "When you make a vow to God, do not delay in fulfilling it. He has no pleasure in fools; fulfill your vow" (Ecclesiastes 5:4).

Yet, I have also had the painful experience of sitting with some of them years later, and the topic has been adultery. At that moment—as they have shared with me the shame and embarrassment of what has taken place, as they struggle to find a way to "put things back together"—there is no passion, no pleasure and no allure left in the idea of an affair, just sorrow and regret. In some cases, to no avail.

At such times, I am reminded of the somber warning from the writer of Hebrews:

> See that no one is sexually immoral, or is godless like Esau, who for a single meal sold his inheritance rights as the oldest son. Afterward, as you know, when he wanted to inherit this blessing, he was rejected. He could bring about no change of mind, though he sought the blessing with tears (Hebrews 12:16-17).

Marriage killers

There are a lot of ways to kill a marriage. If you look at the list of the most commonly stated reasons, money problems is number one, followed closely by incompatibility. Adultery is usually the final step in the death of a marriage, not a first cause.

If I were to try to explain why it is different, I would have to compare it to a deadly disease. Most marriage problems are like cancer. If you catch it early enough, you can treat it. Eventually you can put those "causes" into remission, the health of the marriage can rebound and ultimately be saved.

In contrast, adultery is like committing suicide. Even the most numb mind among us recognizes that adultery is often the death blow to a marriage. Its impact is so devastating to a relationship that it is given in Scripture as the one indisputable justification for divorce.

> It has been said, "Anyone who divorces his wife must give her a certificate of divorce." But I tell you that anyone who divorces his wife, except for marital unfaithfulness, causes her to become an adulteress, and anyone who marries the divorced woman commits adultery (Matthew 5:31-32).

With these words, Jesus was condemning the common practice of his contemporaries of divorcing their wives because they no longer were pleased with them. He told them, there are NO justifiable grounds "except for marital unfaithfulness." We call this an exceptive clause. It excludes all other options for divorce, except this one.

Epidemic?

When couples stand before a minister, family and friends, repeating their vows, they have every intention of keeping them to the letter. Adultery and divorce, hopefully, are the furthest things from their minds. Yet statistical surveys have found that as many as 70 percent of men and 50 percent of women have had at least one adulterous affair in their lifetime. I must admit I find these numbers unbelievably high. Even if we were to cut them in half, they would still include a large number of us.

What is adultery?

The general understanding of the term "adultery" is to engage in voluntary sexual intercourse with someone to whom you are not married. Jesus outlined the principle twice in the Gospel of Matthew:

> But I tell you that anyone who divorces his wife, except for marital unfaithfulness, causes her to become an adulteress, and anyone who marries the divorced woman commits adultery (Matthew 5:32).

> I tell you that anyone who divorces his wife, except for marital unfaithfulness, and marries another woman commits adultery (Matthew 19:9).

Marital unfaithfulness is translated from the Greek word *porneia*, which means any and all "illicit sexual intercourse" such as "adultery, fornication, homosexuality, lesbianism, intercourse with animals, sexual intercourse with close relatives, and/or sexual intercourse with a divorced man or woman."

There have been some who have tried to narrow the definition to justify certain sexual behaviors, but the text is very specific and clear—as Paul declares, "so that they are without excuse" (Romans 1:20).

How does it happen?

As I sit with an individual or couple who are confronting the reality of an affair, I usually begin by asking the guilty party, "How did it happen?" The following are not actual stories but scenarios taken from a number of counseling sessions with couples who have experienced the trauma of infidelity. Together, they form a composite picture of how it happens in many cases.

Scenario for a fall #1

It was an ordinary business trip. Bill had been on them many times before. His plane landed, the shuttle took him to his hotel, he settled into his room. He didn't enjoy these trips. He hated to travel alone. He had made the presentation so many times there wasn't much challenge left in it. He hated the long, lonely nights in a hotel, in a strange city.

After sitting through a "restaurant food" dinner alone, he went back up to his room. He flicked through the channels for a few minutes, not finding anything of interest. Thinking to himself for a few minutes, he decided to take a walk and find something to do.

As stepped out of the elevator into the lobby, he could hear the laughter coming out of the lounge. Bill wasn't a drinker. He didn't know much about bars. The thought of going in intimidated him. Besides, what if he ran into someone he knew, someone from his church? "Nah, that would never happen," he thought, comforting himself. "I'm a thousand miles from home. What harm could it do to go in and have a Coke?"

As Bill entered the lounge, he felt out of place and self-conscious. He sat down in a chair off to the side. Most of the people were either glued to the football game on the TV or engaged in animated conversation about the game.

After a few minutes, the waitress came over to his table and asked him what he would like to drink. He ordered a glass of wine. (After all, doesn't the Bible say a little wine is good for the stomach?) What harm would it do? As he sipped at the wine, he began to relax.

That's when it started. At first he hadn't noticed her. She was sitting with another woman at the other end of the lounge. When his eyes first caught hers, he looked away quickly, pretending that he wasn't staring. She wasn't what you would call beautiful, but she was attractive in an interesting sort of way.

When she first stood up and began to walk in his direction, he assumed that she was leaving. But then she walked up to his table. "You look like you're all alone. Do you mind if I share your company for a few minutes?" She paused for a moment and then extended her hand, "My name is Michelle, what's yours?"

How do you respond to a request like that? You can't just ignore her. You don't want to be rude. Besides, it would be nice to talk to someone. In fact, it would be kind of fun. Nothing was going to come of it. It reminded Bill of when he was in college, always trying to pick-up on girls but never really having much success. If it hadn't been for Karen pursuing him, he probably never would have gotten married. He wasn't too good at meeting girls.

It was a little awkward at first, but a couple more glasses of wine, and Bill started feeling more comfortable. Michelle had a way of making him feel special. He didn't consider himself to be a great conversationalist, but she was so easy to talk to. She laughed at his jokes. She was interested in his stories.

She was at least fifteen years younger than Bill. There were plenty of other young men nearer her age she could have approached, but she commented on how handsome he was, in a mature sort of way. He couldn't remember the last time he had felt attractive to a woman, especially a younger woman.

It was Michelle who first suggested that they go someplace quieter to talk. No one said it, it just seemed natural to go up to her room. She took his arm as they walked out of the lounge. It seemed natural. For a moment Bill wondered if anyone would notice or recognize him . . . but then how could they?

Once in the elevator, she leaned up against him. By the time they got off at her floor, he had his arm around her. They came to her room; she opened the door. Once inside, all pretense was gone. They began to embrace and . . . .

It was only afterward that Bill began to realize what he had done. He didn't even know Michelle's last name. As the next day progressed, he kept on thinking about Karen. What if she found out? What if someone recognized him? What should he do? How could he have done something so stupid?

He decided the best strategy was to just forget the whole thing, as if it had never happened. It was over. Just a fluke. A mistake. No one needed to know. At least that is what he intended until he got home.

As soon as Karen met Bill at the airport, she sensed something wasn't right. She began to probe, asking questions about his trip. Bill tried to deflect her questions, but he didn't do very well. It may have been woman's intuition; Karen finally asked the question, praying that she wouldn't get the answer she feared: "Have you been with another woman?"

Bill lowered his head, and in a barely audible voice, breathed "Yes."

When Bill and Karen first came to me, the signs for reconciliation were hopeful. Neither wanted their marriage to end. But Karen wasn't sure if she could get past what had taken place. She was disappointed and disillusioned. She never thought something like this would ever happen to her and Bill. He wasn't that kind of man, or so she thought.

First of all, could she ever trust Bill again? Because of his job, there would be future trips out of town. The thought of spending days at a time wondering if he would fall again was almost unbearable to anticipate.

Second, there were also questions about how something like this could happen. When a man violates the marriage covenant through infidelity, it is often the woman who assumes a great deal of guilt. She interprets his actions as being a repudiation of her role as his lover and friend. The fact that Michelle had been younger than Karen added to her insecurity. She wondered, was he thinking of the other woman when he had sex with me? Was he comparing?

Karen naturally looked at the event from her point of view. The idea of sleeping with a stranger was totally repugnant to her. Even more incomprehensible to her was that Bill didn't even know Michelle's last name. How could he have had sex with someone he didn't even know? And if his intercourse had been so impersonal with this stranger, what did that say about the times they shared their bodies with one another?

Fortunately, Bill responded to Karen's struggle with a great deal of maturity. He did not seek to shift responsibility to either Karen or Michelle. He had sinned and there was no one to blame but himself.

Second, he allowed Karen to ask any questions she wanted. He tried to answer as honestly and directly as possible. When she got angry, he allowed her to ventilate her anger. He took his punishment. When she became depressed and began to withdraw, he encouraged her to talk about her feelings. As she did, he listened attentively, making every effort to understand.

Third, Bill accepted that the ball was in Karen's court. If the marriage covenant was to be restored, it was her choice. Biblically, she was free to terminate the marriage. She was under no obligation to take him back. I assured him that she needed this sense of free choice if she was going to be able to let go of her anger.

It is my belief that adultery annuls the marriage covenant. It then becomes the prerogative of the innocent spouse to choose whether or not he or she is willing to renew the covenant. I often tell the couple if they choose to renew the covenant, they cannot continue to refer back to the sins of the past. It must be a new beginning.

It took some months for Karen and Bill to turn the corner in the resolution of their relationship, but time heals if we allow it to.

The events of their past will never be totally forgotten, but as Joseph told his brothers who had sold him out of jealousy and bitterness into slavery in Egypt, "You intended to harm me, but God intended it for good . . ." (Genesis 50:20).

Satan had intended to use Bill's sin to destroy his marriage, his family, his testimony and his very life. But our God, who "we know that in all things God works for the good of those who love Him, who have been called according to His purpose" (Romans 8:28), turned disaster into blessing.

Their marriage will never be the same, but it is better.

Scenario for a fall #2

Jim and Janice had been married for almost five years. Theirs wasn't a bad marriage. It just wasn't as good as it once had been. It had been so good in the beginning, but then it just got "ordinary."

They both worked long and hard. When the weekends came, they were pretty tired. They usually slept in late on Saturdays and laid around watching TV on Sundays. Before they knew it, the weekend was over, and it was time to hit the grindstone for another five days.

Neither of them cared for the routine, or "the rut" as they often referred to it, but they had goals they wanted to reach. Their house payments were high; they wanted to do a lot of remodeling; and they needed new furniture. Some day they wanted to start a family. If Janice was going to stay home with the baby, they were going to need to get ahead financially.

The time they spent together wasn't exactly what you would call "quality time." When they were together, they seemed to have a hard time talking, or at least Janice found it hard. Not that she didn't want to talk, but Jim never seemed very interested in what she had to say. When she would tell him about her day, or what happened while she was shopping, he didn't seem to be paying attention. He would acknowledge that she was talking with a grunt or "uh-huh"—not exactly what you would call quality conversation. Most of the time he was either reading or watching TV. Many evenings he would bring work home from the office.

What really bugged her was that he had no trouble talking to his friends. If one of them called, he would go on forever in conversation about stupid stuff like football or golf. When she tried to talk to him about important things like new furniture or spending time together, he would just say, "Do whatever you want, it doesn't matter to me."

To his credit, he did make an effort to buy her nice gifts at Christmas and birthdays. He even had flowers sent to her office on Valentine's Day. She loved to show them off to the other girls in the office, but when she got home, Jim acted as if it was no big deal. It was as if it was just another task on his "to-do" list.

That's when she started to enjoy spending time with Brian. She had known him from work for years. She always acknowledged him in the office, but really didn't pay him much attention. He was younger than she and lacked the kind of ambition and drive that she respected in a man. He wasn't at all like Jim.

One day, during a coffee break, he sat down across from her in the employee lounge. The conversation wasn't anything special, but he seemed genuinely interested when she shared her confusion over the new software program to which the company had converted. He told her he had a pretty good grip on it and if he got a chance would give her a few pointers.

She recalled how she enjoyed the concern he had showed, though she didn't really expect him to follow through. Five years of marriage had taught her a lot about men and their promises. She had been waiting for a year for Jim to fix the leak in the washer. He kept on saying he would get to it first chance he got, after the work week, after the weekend, after the ball game, blah, blah, blah. Every day, she would walk in and look at the same puddle of water.

Janice was genuinely surprised when later that afternoon Brian poked his head over her cubicle, "Is this a good time?" he asked. "Sure," Janice enthusiastically replied. He pulled up a chair next to her and began to walk through the program with her.

She was so impressed with his patience and the gentle way he would correct her when she made an error. It wasn't at all like the impatience and obvious frustration Jim showed when she made a mistake in their checkbook.

Over the next week, Brian continued to check in to see how things were going. As they worked together, she began to find out a lot about him. She discovered that he was a musician and songwriter. She had been wrong about him not being ambitious. This job was just a way of paying the bills while he pursued his real passion, music.

As the weeks went along, they began to meet frequently during coffee breaks. Then one day Janice said, "You know Brian, I never have thanked you for helping me with that program. How about I buy you lunch some time?" Brian said, "Great." After that, Brain and Janice starting having lunch together quite often.

Some of Janice's friends at the office began to notice the time she was spending with Brian, especially when she stopped spending lunch with them. Alice even asked her if something was going on, but Janice laughed and said, "Of course not, we're just friends."

Things had not changed much at home, but it didn't seem to bother Janice as much. She began to see how her friendship with Brian had really helped her marriage. After all, Jim had his friends, and now she had Brian.

Over time, Janice's feelings for Brain began to grow deeper. She still told people that they were just friends, but she began comparing Jim to Brian. Sometimes when she and Jim were in bed, she would fantasize about what it would be like to be with Brian.

One day at the office, Brian mentioned that he had bought a couple of tickets to a concert but then his buddy had to go out of town. Did Janice know of anyone who he could take with him to the concert?

Janice new that Jim would never agree to her going to a concert with "some guy from work." But it sounded like such fun, and she hadn't had any fun in a long time. Besides, nothing was going to happen. They were just friends. She told Brian that she would go with him. She'd meet him there half an hour before the show started.

She got off work early so she could get home ahead of Jim. She wanted to change and put something out for him to eat and then leave a note. That way, he wouldn't ask too many questions. She put something in the note about getting together with some of the girls at work for a baby shower, be home at 11:00 pm.

Janice couldn't remember the last time she had so much fun. It was like being a kid again. After the concert, they went for lattes and talked for about an hour. Brian seemed to know so much about music, musicians, instruments. She was really impressed with both his knowledge and passion for music. He had so much more depth of soul than she had realized, certainly more than Jim.

Then Brian got an idea. "Would you like to see my studio?" It was only a few blocks from the coffee shop. Janice had a slight bit of hesitation, but then she really didn't want this evening to end. So she agreed to go, but just for a few minutes and then she had to get home.

True to her word, Janice stayed only a few minutes. It was already 11:15, and it would be midnight before she got home.

In the months that followed, there were several more secret nights out. Through it all, Janice had very mixed feelings. She really enjoyed the times she spent with Brian, but it really bothered her that Jim never seemed to question why she was out or why she had come home late. Maybe Jim really didn't love her any more. He didn't seem to care.

As her evenings out with Brian continued, they began to become more like dates. One night as they were parting, Janice gave Brian a kiss on the cheek. He responded by giving her a warm embrace. In time, they were holding hands. Eventually they began to meet at his apartment and engage in intercourse.

It wasn't even like Janice could identify a point in time when she crossed the line. It just happened slowly, gradually. One day, she just realized that she didn't love Jim anymore. She loved Brian. She confronted Jim, told him she wanted a divorce and that she wanted him to move out.

When Jim came to me, he was still in a state of shock. He loved his wife and wanted to save his marriage. He didn't know what had happened. He had been a good husband and provider. How could something like this happen?

I made several calls to Janice. Finally, she agreed to talk with me, but she wanted me to know that she had made up her mind and wasn't willing to take Jim back. Eventually, they divorced, and I haven't seen Janice since.

After the breakup, Jim started attending church regularly. Over time, he came to recognize how he had failed to be a caring husband and spiritual leader in his home and repented. He made several more attempts at reconciliation, but by then Janice had become more deeply involved with Brian. He eventually remarried, and he and his new wife just had their first baby.

Brian and Janice eventually moved in together. He had quit his job and was dedicating himself full time to his music career. It was exciting at first for Janice, but over time, it got tiresome. She still worked in order to support Brian's career. He would stay up late working on his music; she would leave early for work. He slept most of the day, since his "gigs" were at night.

She eventually had enough and asked him to leave. He is now living with someone he had been seeing for about six months before he and Janice broke up. Janice now lives alone.

Different motives

There wasn't much I could do for Jim and Janice. Even though Jim was willing, Janice wasn't. In large part, this is due to the difference between the way a woman becomes involved in an affair, in contrast to the man.

Men tend to have more shallow commitments in an affair than do women. In our first story, Bill slept with someone he didn't even know. Janice, on the other hand, took months to develop her attachment. When she finally committed, she was deeply involved emotionally. Her level of commitment to Brian was too high to just walk away.

There is an old adage that states "a cheating man merely strays, but a cheating woman betrays." Men cheat for the sexual and ego gratification it provides. Women cheat to find companionship more than romance. Usually a man can walk away from an affair much more easily than a woman can.

Changing social atmosphere!

Changes in our society have contributed significantly to the increase in adultery. It simply is far easier to cheat on your spouse than it was in past generations.

Counselor and author Gary Collins notes that we live in an age where "emphasis upon immediate, physical, sexual gratification" is all around us. "Media using sex to sell creates a sexually supercharged atmosphere." Michael Campion agrees: "The sexual revolution has developed a hyper, overly stimulated society. Dress (braless), television (jiggle shows), movies (R and X rated), advertising and music are overly sexual."

The effect is to heighten our awareness of sex and exaggerate its importance in our lives. When experts and government officials tell us that we must provide condoms to teens because we can't prevent them from becoming sexually active, they are expressing and validating this distorted attitude.

Americans think more about sex because we deal with

sexual images and thoughts more today than at any other period in our history.

Sexual convenience

Sex has become far more convenient that it was in the past. Contraceptive devices, more effective treatment of sexual disease, abortion and greater social acceptance have all combined to give an impression of sin without consequences.

Of course, the AIDS epidemic has caused some to think twice. Yet we find that many still continue to engage in irresponsible sexual behavior. Why? It is due in large part to the distorted belief that sexual relations lead to happiness, intimacy and true love.

Search for identity and intimacy

For most, the underlying motive for infidelity is identity and intimacy. Men who cheat think their identity is strengthened by an adoring woman. They often see themselves as being romantics. They love infatuation, that fleeting period of passionate romance. It is an illusionary period of time that never, ever lasts. It is founded primarily upon feelings. When the feelings are gone, the romance ends. It is at this point we hear comments like, "I don't know what happened. I just don't love you anymore."

In a marriage, this frequently happens with the birth of the first child. A woman's natural inclination is to center her world on this new member of her family. The baby is totally dependent upon her, and she responds with unlimited care and affection.

Many men become jealous, though they hardly admit it. Before the babies came, they were the center of their wives' world. Now they are viewed more as a partner, sharing in the daily and mundane tasks of caring for the baby. Most wives are too tired caring for a newborn to continue being sexually responsive partners. At this point, it is very common for men to begin looking elsewhere for the adoring affection that has disappeared from their marriages.

A woman, on the other hand, needs to be needed. God

created her to be her husband's counterpart. She is dependent upon his attention and affection to give her an assurance of purpose and significance. When a husband draws back, she is left with an incredible void in her life. Many women will fill this need by becoming absorbed in the lives of their children, but when the children begin to mature, they naturally seek to break away. Eventually, they move out and are no longer dependent upon their parents.

These two factors probably explain why most divorces take place within the first five years or after fifteen years of marriage. The entrance of children often embitters the husband; the departure of the children embitters the wife.

Adultery-proofing your marriage

How does one go about "adultery-proofing" a marriage? Over the years, I have come up with four guidelines that I have found very effective. They are:

1. Don't think it couldn't happen to you.
2. Flee temptation.
3. Fear God and keep His commandments.
4. Count the cost!

"It couldn't happen to me!"

Chuck Smith, Senior Pastor of Calvary Chapel in Costa Mesa, California, once pointed out a principle of spiritual warfare that I have never forgotten. He shared with a group of pastors that we rarely fall in the areas in which we are weak because we tend to be vigilant in those areas. Rather, we are most vulnerable in our areas of strength, for there we fail to adequately protect ourselves, failing to perceive the danger.

Every time I hear someone boast that they would never commit some sin or another, I am reminded of the counsel of the Apostle Paul: "So, if you think you are standing firm, be careful that you don't fall!" (1 Corinthians 10:12). Likewise, Peter warns: "Therefore, dear friends, since you already know this, be on your guard so that you may not be carried away by the error of lawless men and fall from your secure position" (2 Peter 3:17).

Peter warns, these are things "you already know." If we are not on our "guard" we can be "carried away by error" and "fall" from our "secure position" in Christ.

Dr. Billy Graham has become the most respected religious figure in America and much of the world today. This is due in large part to the tremendous success he has had as an international evangelist, but it is also due to the high standard of integrity he has maintained throughout his lifetime.

Early in his ministry he entered into a covenant with his co-laborers in the gospel to establish a code of behavior that would protect them and the ministry. He recognized how easy it would be for one of them to fall. There was a need for limits and to allow others to hold him accountable to these limits.

The result of his commitment is that nothing has ever happened. There has never been the slightest hint or insinuation of impropriety. In an era where sexual scandal has become embarrassingly common, Dr. Graham has maintained a testimony that has protected the reputation of Christ before the unbelievers. The standard of righteousness has been maintained.

The most important protection against falling is recognizing how very vulnerable you are.

Flee temptation!

When temptation comes your way, run the other way!

Abraham Lincoln was once being chided by a critic for not being more aggressive in confronting some of his enemies. He responded by saying, "I have always considered it the wise tack to step aside when confronted by a rabid dog."

The Bible provides similar counsel, when it comes to sin, especially sexual sin:

> Flee from sexual immorality. All other sins a man commits are outside his body, but he who sins sexually sins against his own body (1 Corinthians 6:18).

> Flee the evil desires of youth, and pursue righteousness, faith, love and peace, along with those who call on the Lord out of a pure heart (2 Timothy 2:22).

> Submit yourselves, then, to God. Resist the devil, and he will flee from you (James 4:7).

Compare this advice from scripture with the story of King David's adultery with Bathsheba:

> In the spring, at the time when kings go off to war, David sent Joab out with the king's men and the whole Israelite army. They destroyed the Ammonites and besieged Rabbah. But David remained in Jerusalem. One evening David got up from his bed and walked around on the roof of the palace. From the roof he saw a woman bathing. The woman was very beautiful, and David sent someone to find out about her. The man said, "Isn't this Bathsheba, the daughter of Eliam and the wife of Uriah the Hittite?" Then David sent messengers to get her. She came to him, and he slept with her. (She had purified herself from her uncleanness.) Then she went back home. The woman conceived and sent word to David, saying, "I am pregnant" (2 Samuel 11:1-5).

Does David flee temptation? No! He sees a woman bathing. Does he turn his eyes or depart? No, he gazes at her long enough to recognize that she is very beautiful. He watches her long enough to allow an impure desire to grow. Then he inquires about her. The fact that she is another man's wife does not matter to him. His voyeurism has overtaken him.

There was no consideration of consequences. But consequences did come, and they were terrible. Because of his sin, he lost three sons; his daughter Tamar was raped by her half-brother; he temporarily lost his kingdom and was shamed before the entire nation. These were the consequence of God's judgment against David, as declared by the prophet Nathan: "Now, therefore, the sword shall never depart from your house, because you despised me and took the wife of Uriah the Hittite to be your own" (2 Samuel 12:10).

Fear God and keep His commandments

One of the elements missing in the story of David and Bathsheba is any reference to the fear of God on David's part. In the heat of passion, his thoughts were only upon the gratification of his own passions. God's power and pleasure were lost in the heat of the moment.

Contrast David's failure with Joseph's glorious stand against temptation. When Potiphar's wife seeks to entice him into sexual immorality, he rebuffs her declaring,

> No one is greater in this house than I am. My master has withheld nothing from me except you, because you are his wife. How then could I do such a wicked thing and sin against God? (Genesis 39:9).

The fear of God is both a worshipful reverence and a terror of falling under God's judgment. Those who fear God recognize that He does not wink at sin but holds all men accountable, especially those who profess faith in Christ.

Not surprisingly, it was Solomon, the son of King David, who gave one of the strongest exhortations in the Bible against adultery. He had seen firsthand the terrible consequences of this sin. Listen to his words of warning:

> For the prostitute reduces you to a loaf of bread, and the adulteress preys upon your very life. Can a man scoop fire into his lap without his clothes being burned? Can a man walk on hot coals without his feet being scorched? So is he who sleeps with another man's wife; no one who touches her will go unpunished. Men do not despise a thief if he steals to satisfy his hunger when he is starving. Yet if he is caught, he must pay sevenfold, though it costs him all the wealth of his house. But a man who commits adultery lacks judgment; whoever does so destroys himself. Blows and disgrace are his lot, and his shame will never be wiped away; for jealousy arouses a husband's fury, and he will show no mercy when he takes revenge. He will not accept any compensation; he will refuse the bribe, however great it is (Proverbs 6:26-35).

I regret to say that more than once I have seen this warning literally fulfilled in the lives of men I have personally known and loved. These are not just words of advice from an ancient book. These are Words of God. They have divine force. As Isaiah the prophet stated, ". . . so is my word that goes out from my mouth: It will not return to me empty, but will accomplish what I desire and achieve the purpose for which I sent it" (Isaiah 55:11).

Count the cost!

Years ago, I came across the following in a publication. The original was credited to Randy Alcorn. I have changed it slightly to be more descriptive of my own situation. It was entitled, Consequences of a Moral Tumble. As you read it, I would encourage you to personalize for yourself, as I have.

Whenever I feel particularly vulnerable to sexual temptation, I find it helpful to review what effects my action could have:

Grieving the Lord who redeemed me.

Dragging His sacred name into the mud.

One day having to look at Jesus, the Righteous Judge, in the face and give an account of my actions.

Following in the footsteps of these people whose immorality forfeited their ministries and caused me to shudder (list names).

Inflicting untold hurt on Jamie, my best friend and loyal wife.

Losing Jamie's respect and trust.

Hurting my beloved children: Beth, Ben, Britt and Brian.

Destroying my example and credibility with my children and nullify both present and future efforts to teach them to obey God. ("Why listen to a man who betrayed Mom and us?")

If my blindness should continue or my wife be unable to forgive me, perhaps losing my wife and my children forever.

Causing shame to my family. ("Why isn't Daddy a pastor anymore?")

Losing self-respect.

Creating a form of guilt awfully hard to shake. Even though God would forgive me, would I forgive myself?

Forming memories and flashbacks that could plague future intimacy with my wife.

Wasting years of ministry training and experience for a long time, maybe permanently.

Forfeiting the effect of years of witnessing to my family.

Undermining the faithful example and hard work of other Christians in our community.

Bringing great pleasure to Satan, the enemy of God and all that is good.

Heaping judgment and endless difficulty on the person with whom I committed adultery.

Possibly bearing the physical consequences of such diseases as gonorrhea, syphilis, chlamydia, herpes, and AIDS; perhaps infecting Jamie or, in the case of AIDS, even causing her death.

Possibly causing pregnancy, with the personal and financial implications, including a lifelong reminder of my sin.

Bringing shame and hurt to my fellow pastors, elders and staff members.

Causing shame and hurt to close friends, especially those I've led to Christ and discipled.

Invoking shame and life-long embarrassment upon myself.

If every man and woman who has ever fallen into adultery had first stopped to give this kind of careful analysis to the real effects of their sin, it is not likely that many would have yielded to temptation.

13

The Power Of Hope

[I had fainted], unless I had believed to see the goodness of the LORD in the land of the living. Wait on the LORD: be of good courage, and he shall strengthen thine heart: wait, I say, on the LORD. (Psalm 27: 13,14 KJV).

Several years ago, one of the old S-4 class of submarines was rammed by another ship off the coast of Massachusetts. It quickly sank. The entire crew was trapped in its prison house of death. Ships rushed to the scene of the disaster, and although the situation was hopeless, still Navy divers were dispatched to see if there was any way possible to effect a rescue. Finally one of them reached the hull of the damaged submarine. As he placed his helmeted ear to the side of the vessel and listened, he heard a tapping noise. Someone, he discovered, was tapping out a question in the dots and dashes of Morse Code. The question came slowly: "Is . . . there . . . any . . . hope?" Tragically there wasn't. The entire crew perished.

The importance of hope

What effect does hope have upon the way we live our lives? As I ask the question, I am reminded of a research project conducted several years ago. The purpose of the study was to identify why some people are able to endure various hardships for long periods of time, while others seem to give up rather quickly, even though they are facing the same problems with the same available resources.

Rats were used for the experiment. The researchers began by placing these rats in a large tank of water. The sides of the tank were very steep and smooth, so it was impossible for the rats to climb out unaided by the researchers. Once dropped into the water, the rats began swimming around feverishly, moving quickly around the rim of the tank, looking for a means of escape. Because there was no way out, they soon began to tire. After about 15 minutes, the rats would give up and sink to the bottom of the tank.

At that very moment, one of the researchers would pluck the drowning rat out of the tank, dry it off, warm it up, and then allow it to rest for several minutes. Once the rat had regained its strength, again the researchers would drop it back into the water.

Like before, the rat would resume swimming around the tank. But instead of trying to climb out, they waited to be rescued, as before. They continued to swim for two, sometimes three hours before giving up in exhaustion.

Why this difference? In a word, it was "HOPE." In the first instance, the rats' endurance faded as they realized that their circumstance was hopeless. But once they had experienced rescue at the hands of laboratory workers, they pressed on until they were completely physically spent.

We can't live without hope!

You see, it is hope that sustains us. Samuel Johnson once wrote, "The natural flights of the human mind are not from pleasure to pleasure but from hope to hope."

Again, this is well illustrated by a survey taken by psychologist William Marston. He asked 3000 people, "What have you to live for?" He was shocked to discover that 94 percent were simply enduring the present while they waited for the future. Some simply responded that they were "waiting for something to happen . . . waiting for next year, waiting for a better time, waiting for someone to die, waiting for tomorrow . . . " Essentially, their entire purpose for living was the hopeful expectation of some future good.

At Fairchild Air Force Base, outside of Spokane, Washington, the Air Force maintains their winter survival school. Here airmen are trained and tested to survive in cold climates, living off the land, by their wits, and evading capture.

I attended a tour of the facility a few years ago. The survival instructor who gave us the tour made a fascinating comment. He stated that they had discovered the following about survival in the harsh winter climates of the northwest: "A man can live for three months without shelter; three weeks without food; three days without water; three minutes without air. But he can't survive three seconds without hope."

Is there hope for my marriage?

Over the years, as I have talked with many couples and individuals about their marriages, one critical question has been most often asked of me: "Pastor, is there any hope?"

My response is always the same. If two people are willing to commit to do whatever it takes to make a marriage work, there is always hope. Marriages die because one or both of the people involved give up hope and stop trying to make it work. I don't say this theoretically. I have seen it proven in many marriages. I have worked with couples who came to me with problems I believed were unsolvable. And yet, because they were willing to work on their marriage, God was able to minister His healing grace to their relationship. Our God specializes in doing the impossible. Jesus constantly reminded the disciples (and us) of this fact:

> I tell you the truth, if you have faith as small as a mustard seed, you can say to this mountain, "Move from here to there," and it will move. Nothing will be impossible for you (Matthew 17:20).

> Jesus looked at them and said, "With man this is impossible, but with God all things are possible" (Matthew 19:26).

> For nothing is impossible with God (Luke 1:37).

Conversely, I have seen couples whose marriages were not in that bad of shape, but one or both had decided it would be too hard or take too long to restore, so they just quit trying. They use phrases like "irreconcilable differences" to explain their lack of effort. Some have even told me that it wasn't God's will for them to be married in the first place and that is why their marriage was unhappy. Regardless of what explanations they use, it all comes down to the same thing: they just quit ... just like the rats. They lost hope, gave up, and the marriage drowned in neglect, conflict and hostility.

Little Annie

I am sure you are familiar with the story of Helen Keller. Born a deaf-mute, she was considered uneducable, totally incorrigible, and was destined for life in an institution.

But have you ever heard the story of "Little Annie"? Some years before the birth of Helen Keller, in a mental institution outside Boston, a young girl known as "Little Annie" was locked in the dungeon. The reason behind such inhumane treatment seemed obvious to those charged with caring for her. In many ways, Little Annie was like an animal. On occasion, she would violently attack others. At other times, she would completely ignore them, as if she were unable to notice them—totally unresponsive. The dungeon was the only place, in the opinion of the doctors, for those who were hopelessly insane. This was common treatment for such people over a hundred years ago.

In Little Annie's case, they saw no hope for her, so she was consigned to a living death in that small cage which received little light and even less hope.

About that time, an elderly nurse was nearing retirement. For reason of compassion known only to her, she started taking her lunch into the dungeon and eating outside Little Annie's cage. She felt perhaps she should communicate some love and hope to the little girl.

At first, when the elderly nurse started visiting her, Little Annie gave no indication that she was even aware of her presence. One day, the elderly nurse brought some brownies to the dungeon and left them outside the cage. Little Annie gave no hint she knew they were there, but when the nurse returned the next day, the brownies were gone. From that time on, the nurse would bring brownies when she made her Thursday visit.

Soon after, the doctors in the institution noticed a change was taking place. After a period of time, they decided to move Little Annie upstairs. Finally, the day came when the "hopeless case" was told she could return home. But Little Annie did not wish to leave. She chose to stay, to help others. It was she who cared for, taught, and nurtured Helen Keller. Her name was Anne Sullivan.

Expectation or anticipation

As I read through the New Testament, I notice something quite interesting. God never tells us to live in expectation but in anticipation. It may not be apparent to you that there is a difference between these two words, but there is. "Expectation" comes when we are looking forward to some goal or objective. We can already picture it in our mind. We may work toward it or wait for it to be given to us. But often in life, our expectations are disappointed. Both people and circumstance let us down. Often, the result is depression, or as Solomon put it, "Hope deferred maketh the heart sick . . ." (Proverbs 13:12, KJV).

"Anticipation" is similar to expectation, except with one vital difference. Whereas expectation is looking forward to something in particular, anticipation does not know exactly what it is looking forward to. Anticipation rests on the love and goodness of God. The Apostle John explains it this way:

> Dear friends, now we are children of God, and what we will be has not yet been made known. But we know that when he appears, we shall be like him, for we shall see him as he is (1 John 3:2).

When my children were small, I always made it a point to purchase them a gift whenever I traveled. I would usually stop at the gift shop in whatever airport I happened to be passing through on my journey. My kids never knew what I was going to bring them. They just knew that Daddy always brought them a gift. They would await my arrival with great excitement. When they received their gift, they always received it with joy and appreciation. They awaited my return with anticipation.

Again, this is what Paul describes in writing to both the Corinthians and the Ephesians:

> However, as it is written: No eye has seen, no ear has heard, no mind has conceived what God has prepared for those who love him (1 Corinthians 2:9).

> Now to him who is able to do immeasurably more than all we ask or imagine, according to his power that is at work within us (Ephesians 3:20).

As followers of Christ, it is not always possible to know what to expect from God because, "How unsearchable His judgments, and His paths beyond tracing out!" (Romans 11:33). In truth, we can only live in "anticipation" of the good He is going to bring to pass in our lives.

As my children got older, they began to make specific requests for certain items. If I was able to procure these items, then they were happy. Why? Because their expectations had been met. But if I was unable to find what they had requested, then they were disappointed.

In a sense, this is what happens to most of us when we get married. We enter marriage with certain expectations of how it is going to be. Rarely, if ever, do our illusions about marriage turn out to be accurate. What follows is disillusionment.

What we need to begin to realize is that God has something better in store for us than we are even able to comprehend. Even though we may not see it, God has specifically chosen this person to be our life's companion, so the interaction and interchange that will take place between us will accomplish His work of shaping and molding in our lives. Proverbs 27:17 describes the process this way: "As iron sharpens iron, so one man sharpens another." The "friction" which we try to avoid in our relationships with others is often the very tool God uses to "sharpen" our hearts and minds for His purposes. If you see God working in the conflicts and struggles of life, you will have joy based upon your anticipation of the good which He will certainly bring. If you don't believe that your circumstance has anything to do with God, then you will be disappointed, frustrated, even angry. You will seek to find a way out. You will lose hope.

But "hope" in the goodness of God is one of the distinguishing characteristics of the Christian. As Paul reminded the Ephesians:

> Therefore, remember that formerly you who are Gentiles by birth and called "uncircumcised" by those who call themselves "the circumcision" (that done in the body by the hands of men)—remember that at that time you were separate from Christ, excluded from citizenship in Israel and foreigners to the covenants of the promise, without hope and without God in the world. But now in Christ Jesus you who once were far away have been brought near through the blood of Christ (Ephesians 2:11-13).

A matter of perspective

Somewhere along the line, we have concluded that, because the Bill of Rights states that the government's duty is to guarantee my freedom to "pursue" whatever I believe will contribute most to my personal happiness, I should always be happy.

Happiness is not a birthright. It isn't even ostensibly an emotion or feeling. Really, it is a state of mind. I often like to illustrate this by a story I heard many years ago about two identical twins. One was an extreme optimist, the other an extreme pessimist. The first saw a silver lining around every cloud, no matter how dark. The other could see nothing good no matter how favorable the circumstance. The story goes like this:

> Once there was a family with two young boys with extremely different personalities. One was an extreme optimist; the other an extreme pessimist.
>
> The parents of these two boys decided they needed to do something to balance out these extremes in their children's personalities, for the older they got, the more extreme their behaviors became.
>
> After trying many different techniques and consulting with a variety of specialists, they were about to give up when they heard about a clinic specially designed to address and correct such personality disorders.
>
> After assessing the two children, the doctors prescribed a treatment they were sure would work. First, they led the pessimistic child to a room filled with every toy and game a

child of his age could possibly dream about. They locked him in this room overnight to see how this would affect his point of view. Then they placed the second child, the uncontrollable optimist, in a room filled with nothing but horse manure. They reasoned that after seeing the toys in the first room, and then spending a night sitting in a pile of horse manure, this would certainly breed a little pessimism into this otherwise optimistic child.

Early the next morning, the doctors hurried to the locked rooms to see the results of their therapy. Slowly, they opened the first door and peaked in. There, sitting in the middle of the room, surrounded by piles of broken toys, was the pessimistic child. He was systematically breaking every toy, all the time muttering about what "pieces of junk" they were.

This was discouraging. But they were certain that second child would show better results. When they opened the door to the second room, they were stunned by what they saw. The optimistic child was running in circles in the manure. Occasionally, he would reach down and grab a handful of manure and throw it in the air, followed by a shout of glee. When they finally managed to slow him down and get him settled, they asked him what he was so happy about. He immediately blurted out, "When you've got this much manure, there's got to be a pony somewhere!"

Hang in there!

My parents never had what one could call a good marriage. They were not believers and lacked the support of the church, the Word and the Lord, but they managed to stay married for 39 years.

There is one day that stands out clearly in my mind as I think about my parents' marriage. I was fourteen years old, a sophomore in high school. We had just arrived at the boarding school my older brother was attending. He was in his senior year.

After getting my brother settled in, the four of us sat in the car visiting before saying good-bye. Then it happened. My dad's tone of voice changed and got very solemn and serious. "Boys," he began, "your mother and I have decided to get a divorce."

I was so stunned I was unable to speak. My brother, on the other hand, began to lobby furiously to persuade my parents to change their minds. My parents made no effort to refute his arguments, they just listened.

The issue was never brought up to us again. Years later, my mother told me that she and my father had decided that the impact of a divorce would be too painful for their boys. They stuck together for our sakes.

I know that the contemporary opinion is that it would have been better for them to have separated. I totally disagree. Their marriage never got much better. But I am forever grateful to them for showing the willingness to sacrifice their own desires for our sakes. By their staying together, they enabled my brother and I to grow up with the emotional and economic security of a stable family. We didn't have to go through any of the chaos and confusion of step-relatives, custody, support and the like. I also believe that it contributed considerably to my own determination not to divorce when my marriage went through difficult times. It has been well established that children who grow up in divorced homes are far more likely to choose that avenue in dealing with unhappy marriages. After all, it is the model that is lived out before them.

What's in it for me?

As much as most of us like to think of ourselves as being altruistic, the truth is we are motivated by personal benefit. The tricky part is determining truly what is in my best interests, both in the short and long term.

Too many of us live for immediate gratification. We think only in terms of today, next week, or next month. If our marriage is in a painful period, we only think about escaping the pain as quickly as possible. It rarely occurs to us that the pain is part of God's greater plan for our life, along the lines as the Apostle Paul understood it:

> For our light and momentary troubles are achieving for us an eternal glory that far outweighs them all (2 Corinthians 4:17).

Paul interpreted his sufferings and hardships in light of Christ's ultimate kingdom and the ability such difficulties instilled in those who endured them.

> Praise be to the God and Father of our Lord Jesus Christ, the Father of compassion and the God of all comfort, who comforts us in all our troubles, so that we can comfort those in any trouble with the comfort we ourselves have received from God. For just as the sufferings of Christ flow over into our lives, so also through Christ our comfort overflows. If we are distressed, it is for your comfort and salvation; if we are comforted, it is for your comfort, which produces in you patient endurance of the same sufferings we suffer. And our hope for you is firm, because we know that just as you share in our sufferings, so also you share in our comfort (2 Corinthians 1:3-7).

One of the most liberating days in my life was when I began to view my marital struggles with the above perspective. I wasn't just having marriage problems, I was suffering for Christ. I was enduring hardships as a good soldier of Jesus Christ (2 Timothy 2:3). And as I endured, I was gaining insights and compassion that would enable me to someday minister and encourage others who would go through the same trials.

This book is the testimony of the fulfillment of the above Scripture. Over the years, I have seen thousands of couples who have been encouraged, corrected and healed through the things I have shared. Just recently, I sat down with a pastor and his wife who were going through some hard places in their marriage. As the wife shared her struggles, I was able to identify with them because my wife and I had gone through the very same conflicts. When she learned that her struggles were normal in the context of the pastoral marriage, that alone lifted a ton of pressure off her shoulders. She wasn't weird because she had these thoughts, feelings, frustrations and conflicts. They were not the evidence of her failure as a pastor's wife. Rather, they were the natural challenges of life in the "fishbowl" of ministry and all the spiritual warfare that comes with it.

Four good reasons to hang in there

Over the years, I have come up with a short list of good reasons why someone should labor to stay married.

1. God's best for your children: If you have children, it is one of the best gifts you can give them. God has designed them with an inherent need for their biological parents to be the primary people in their lives. This is usually God's best for both the parents and the children.

2. God's best for our nation: As I documented earlier, society benefits from "whole" families. If society is to be stable and peaceful, it needs the enculteration process that can only happen in the family.

3. God's best for His kingdom: The gospel finds its witness in more than just the words we speak. It is also validated by the lives we live. Many of us in the ministry know the difficulty in preaching to those who have become cynical about Christianity because of the dysfunctional lives of so many who claim to be followers of Christ. If for no other reason, we should do everything in our power to strengthen our own families so the Gospel will not be hindered in the lives of those who are watching us every day.

4. God's best for you: Lastly, a healthy marriage is God's best for you. It is worth fighting for and hanging on to, because in the end, doing God's will always results in the greatest benefit for us. As the writer of Hebrews exhorts, "Let us not become weary in doing good, for at the proper time we will reap a harvest if we do not give up" (Galatians 6:9). After 25 years of marriage, I believe this to be true more than ever.

In closing, I leave you with the contemplation of the words of King David. I pray that you will hold them to be true for your life and your marriage.

> I had fainted, unless I had believed to see the goodness of the LORD in the land of the living. Wait on the LORD: be of good courage, and he shall strengthen thine heart: wait, I say, on the LORD (Psalms 27:13,14, KJV).

Selah!

Bibliography

1. Webster's Encyclopedic Unabridged Dictionary of the English Language, (Portland House, New York, 1989).

2. Spiros Zodhiates, *Happy or Blessed?*, (Ministries Today, Jan/Feb 1987, pg. 13).

3. H. Norman Wright, Marital Counseling: A Biblically Based, Behavioral, Cognitive Approach, (Denver, Colorado, 1981, pg. 10).

4. Born Again: A Look at Christians in America, (The Barna Research Group, Glendale, California, 1990.)

5. Richard Dobbins, *Divorce's Impact on Young People*, (Ministries Today, March/April, 1990, pg. 44).

6. Bob Welch, *When Couples Say I Don't* (Focus on the Family, April 1992), ppg. 10-11).

7. Chuck Swindoll, The Quest for Character, (Multnomah Press Inc., Portland, Oregon, 1990).

8. The Church Today: Insightful Statistics and Commentary, (Barna Research Group, Glendale, California, 1990).

9. William Wilson, New Wilson's Old Testament Word Studies, (Grand Rapids: Kregal Publications, 1987, pg. 215).

10. Webster's Encyclopedic Unabridged Dictionary of the English Language, (New York: Portland House, 1989).

11. James Mallory, The Kink and I. (Wheaton, IL: Victor Books, 1976).

12. *Men vs Women*, (U.S. News and World Report, 105:50-7, August 8, 1988.)

13. Alfred Edershim, The Life and Times of Jesus the Messiah. (W.B. Eerdmans Publishing Co., Grand Rapids, Michigan, Nov. 1971).

14. W. E. Vine, An Expository Dictionary of New Testament Words, (Fleming H. Revell Co., 1965, pg. 58).

15. Bill Hybels, Who Are You When No One Is Looking. (Intervarsity Press, Dovers Grove, Illinois, 1987).

16. Wuest's Word Studies from the Greek New Testament, 1 Peter, Vol. 2 (Wm. B. Eerdmans Publishing Co., Grand Rapids, Mich, n.d., ppg. 75-76).

17. Ibid., pg. 78.

18. Gene Getz, The Measure of the Family, (Glendale, CA: Regal Books Division, G/L Publishers, n.d.).

19. Jamieson, Fausset and Brown, Commentary on the Whole Bible, (Grand Rapids: Zondervan Publishing House, n.d.).

20. Ibid.

21. W. E. Vine, An Expository Dictionary of New Testament Words , (Fleming H. Revell Co. 1965).

22. George Gilder, Men and Marriage (Gretna: Pelican Press Co., 1986).

23. Key Ebling, The Failure of Feminism, (Newsweek, November 19, 1990, pg. 9).

24. William Barclay, The Acts of the Apostles, (The Westminister Press, Philadelphia, n.d., ppg. 28,29).

25. Bill Hybels, Christians in a Sex Crazed Culture , (Victor Books, Wheaton, Ill., n.d.).

26. C.S. Lewis, The Four Loves. (Harvest Books, New York, NY, 1971).

27. Time, The Weekly News Magazine, (Copyright Time Inc., 1975, Time 106: 9, September, 1975, pg 62).

28. Dr. Willard F. Harley, His Needs /Her Needs , (Fleming H. Revell, Grand Rapids, Michigan. 1986).

29. Ken Hamel, The Online Bible, (Woodside Bible Fellowship, Oakhurst, NJ, 1993).

Study Guide

Most of us understand that the more time you spend thinking about something, the deeper your understanding of it. Conversely, we have all had the experience of reading a book, or attending a seminar, and soon afterward forgetting most of what we have heard.

This study guide is designed to help you gain a deeper insight and application of teachings found in this book. Hopefully, it will help to keep the issues and needed "change-points" clearly and firmly before your gaze. At the very least, it will serve as an on-going reminder of the things you have learned.

This guide consists of four parts:

Part one is **On your own,** and consists of a Bible reading followed by a few key questions related to that reading.

Part two is called **Give it some deeper thought.** The purpose of this section is to help you both reflect on what you have read in the specific chapters of each section.

Part three I have called **Get together and talk about it.** These are questions designed to be used in small group discussions.

Part four is **Putting it into action.** These are suggestions to help you put some of the truth you have gained into action.

Session #1: To Be Happy or Holy?
(Chapters 1 & 2)

On your own . . .

Find it in the Bible . . . Begin by reading the Beatitudes located in Matthew 5:1-16. Then, answer the following questions:

1. What is the difference between the words "blessed" and our popular conception of being "happy"?

2. Make a list of the behaviors Jesus says will lead to a "blessed" life. Do these sound like the kinds of things you enjoy doing? Next to your list of behaviors, write the rewards that will follow each.

Behavior	Reward
"poor in spirit"	"theirs is the kingdom"

Give it some deeper thought . . .

The best things that have happened in my life have not always been the happiest. For example, the three best things that have ever happened to me were, in order:
1) The day I received Christ as my Savior.
2) The day I married my sweetheart.
3) The day I became a father.

Unfortunately, those were not the happiest days of my life, because I did not know then what I know now. Instead, each of these events was a terrifying, life-changing step in my life.

In retrospect, they were the best decisions of my life because of their wonderfully positive effect.

What are the three most momentous decisions you have made in your life? (The ones that have brought the greatest blessings?) Were they also the happiest moments?

Get together and talk about it . . .

1. The painful effects of divorce have touched each of us. What are some of the negative effects you have seen or experienced?

2. What do you feel is the primary reason so many marriages in America fail?

3. What advice would you give to someone who is considering divorce as a solution to an unhappy marriage?

4. Why does the Bible so strongly warn against divorce?

Putting it into action . . .

When you pronounced your marriage vows, you stated you would stay with your spouse till "death do you part." Reaffirm that commitment first to God, then to yourself. Then, share with your spouse your commitment to remain faithful for the rest of your life.

Session #2: Incompatible by Design
(Chapters 3 & 4)

On your own . . .

Begin by reading Genesis, chapters 2 and 3. Then, answer the following questions:

1. What (who) is the centerpiece of God's creation?

2. Everything in God's creation is "good" except for one thing. What is it?

3. What were the three reasons Genesis gives for the creation of woman?

4. Genesis, chapter three, reveals the root cause of all marital problems (as well as everything else that is wrong in the world). What is this root cause to all human sorrow and suffering?

5. What six effects does sin have upon human relationships? List the places in Genesis 3 where each effect is identified.

Give it some deeper thought . . .

God first instituted marriage in the idyllic environment of the Garden of Eden. What made Eden utopian was the absence of sin.

It is worthy of noting that marriage was never created to function within a sinful environment. Before sin entered human history, Adam and Eve had a perfect relationship (Genesis 2:25). But after sin, their relationship began to fall apart.

Have you ever given thought to the role which sin plays in your marital conflicts? Have you ever considered the role of spiritual warfare (Satanic influence) upon your marriage?

Have you ever recognized the need to repent to God after you have had an argument with your spouse?

Take a few moments to think about the role that sin has had in your marriage. Identify some areas of specific sinfulness (e.g. pride, anger, bitterness, and lust) that have negatively affected your relationship with your spouse. Then confess them to God, and your spouse, if necessary.

Get together and talk about it . . .

1. Emotionally, every successful marriage goes through three phases: Illusion (we also call this infatuation), Dis-Illusion (when the smoke clears and we begin to see who we really married), and Enrichment (when we decide to love unconditionally the one we married, warts and all). Briefly describe how you passed through these three phases.

2. How has God used your spouse as a "helper" in your marriage?

3. Identify some basic ways in which you and your spouse are inherently different. How has this led to conflict? How have those differences contributed to your personal growth?

Putting it into action . . .

Has it ever occurred to you that God has purposely put you and your spouse together so He could use your spouse to expose and smooth off some of your rough edges?

We tend to focus only on the negative feelings, ignoring the positive effects. Identify one area of your personality or character which has been positively changed as a result of your spouse. Then tell them thanks!

Session #3: Loving Unconditionally
(Chapters 5 & 6)

On your own . . .

Begin by reading Ephesians 5:21-33. Then, answer the following questions:

1. Paul's letter to the church in Ephesus is divided into two major sections: Chapters 1-3 are a doctrinal discussion of the basis of our relationship with Christ; Chapters 4-6 are a practical application of that doctrine to our relationship with others.

In his discussion, Paul moves from generalities to specifics, until in 5:21 he begins to focus upon the three primary relationships in our lives: Marriage, Family and Job.

In each of these three areas he gives specific instructions for how we should treat and respond to one another. Make a list of how we are to respond in each relationship.

In Marriage:

Husbands   Wives

In the Family:

Parents   Children

On the Job:

Employer   Employee

Give it some deeper thought . . .

Philippians 2:5-9 describes the "attitude" which Jesus had toward life in general and people in particular. How does His attitude compare to the way you view yourself and others?

If you were consistently to behave in the manner described here by Paul, what kind of impact would that have upon your marriage?

Take a few moments to think about it and then write down how you would deal differently with your next conflict.

Get together and talk about it . . .

1. Women often complain Paul was picking on women when he wrote about marriage in Ephesians 5. Yet, if you study the passage closely, you would see that this is hardly the case. Who do you think has the tougher responsibility? The man or the woman? Why?

2. Why do you think Paul instructs women to "submit" and men to "love"? Are they really all that different? Or are they looking at the same behavior from differing perspectives?

3. In your opinion, what is the ultimate goal or purpose of marriage? Does your opinion agree or differ with what Paul says is the ultimate purpose?

Putting it into action . . .

The key to a fulfilled relationship is mutual submission. Women submit to their husbands by showing them respect and support for their authority and leadership. Men submit to their wives by loving them sacrificially.

Focus on things you can do to make your spouse's life easier, rather than thinking about how they might make yours easier.

Session #4: Adding Value
(Chapters 7 & 8)

_____**On your own . . .**_____

Begin by reading 1 Peter 2:13-3:9. Then answer the following questions.

1. What is the theme of this section of 1 Peter? Do not let the chapter separations mislead. Read through the entire section, remembering the verse and chapter divisions were not in the original. This will help you maintain the context.

2. Make an outline of this section:
    Introductory premise:
    I.
    II.
    III.
    Closing exhortation:

3. Peter warns against using our "freedom" as a "cover-up" for evil (2:16). What are some of the ways Peter sees slaves, wives and husbands of being guilty of this libertine attitude?

    a. "Slave" (2:18-25)

    b. "Wives" (3:1-6)

    c. "Husbands" (3:7)

4. In the last three verses of this section, Peter lists attitudes/ behaviors, which can build relationships and those that can destroy them. Make a list of each.

                Build   Destroy

Give it some deeper thought . . .

On page 119, I speak about "adding value." This concept is illustrated scripturally by the illustration of the "potter and the clay." What the Bible writers are telling us is that God is seeking to "add value" to our lives by shaping and molding us after the image of His Son.

In Ephesians 5:1 and 1 Thessalonians 2:14, Paul exhorts us to be "imitators of God." Therefore, as I grow and mature in my faith, I should be attempting to "add value" to others.

Take a moment to ask yourself, "In what ways have I been 'adding value' to my wife? To my children? To my friends?"

Get together and talk about it . . .

1. We hear it often: Opposites Attract! Do you believe that is true? In what ways are you and your spouse similar? In what ways are you dissimilar?

2. I have found that the "differences" between our spouses and us are often the things that initially attract us to them. Ironically, they also become the things we find most irritating about them. Why do you think this is?

3. I believe that God causes opposites to attract on purpose. Do you agree? What positive purpose do you think this difference serves? How does it help us to grow in Christ?

Putting it into action . . .

Identify the most difficult area for you to submit/lead in, as a wife/husband. Ask God to help you begin to trust Him, instead of distrusting your spouse. Also, ask Him to enable you to change this area of weakness and sin in your life.

Purpose to give your spouse the opportunity to grow in this area without your criticism or correction.

Session #5: Who's In Charge?
(Chapters 9 & 10)

On your own . . .

Begin by reading 1 Corinthians 11:3-16. Then answer the following:

1. In the above passage, Paul speaks about men needing to have their heads "uncovered" when they pray, worship or teach in the public assemblies and for women to be "covered." He also states that it is a shame for a man to have "long hair," like that of a woman.

This practice would have been in direct opposition and contradiction to the common Jewish and pagan practices of the day, where both men and women covered their heads in public worship ceremonies.

Is this passage primarily about head coverings, or is Paul speaking about a more basic issue? What do you think the issue is?

2. How would you explain the application of this teaching to our world today? What is the crux of Paul's message?

Give it some deeper thought . . .

We are all influenced, to one degree or another, by the culture in which we live. Yet, most of us have given very little thought to what degree and in which ways we have been influenced by non-Christian world views.

How have modern feminist philosophies and rhetoric affected your view of the authority issue in your home? Is your view of the husband-wife relationship biblical?

Get together and talk about it . . .
---

1. Many feminists have accused the Apostle Paul of being an oppressor of women because of his teachings on authority in the home and church. Do you believe this is a fair and accurate appraisal?

2. Why do you think the issue of leadership in the marriage and family is such a difficult and often divisive issue?

3. Why do you think many men are confused about their roles in the marriage and family today?

4. Why do you think so many women are afraid to relinquish leadership to their husbands?

Putting it into action . . .

A big part of respect for authority is sharing information. Does your spouse know why you do what you are doing? Many times I have found that couples keep secrets from each other.

Set a time once a week to talk about all the important areas of your family life: finances, child-rearing, scheduling, etc. Solicit and listen to each other's thoughts and concerns.

In so doing, you can begin to establish a working relationship. And wives, let your husband make the final decision. This may be a little scary in the beginning, but by doing so you are encouraging him to assume leadership responsibility.

If you think his decision is wrong, tell him so graciously. If he will not listen, pray for him and leave it in God's hands.

Session #6: Fun and Faithfulness in Marriage!
(Chapters 11 & 12)

On your own . . .

Begin by reading Song of Solomon 4:1-16 & Hebrews 13:4. Then answer the following:

1. Many have concluded that God has a negative view of sexuality and romance in marriage. Is this borne out by how the topic is dealt with in the Bible?

2. If sexuality is not condemned in the Bible, what is the sexual behavior which is condemned?

3. According to the Bible, what is the single most effective way to avoid sexual immorality? (1 Corinthians 6:18; 2 Timothy 2:22; James 4:7)

4. What does the Bible warn are some of the consequences of sexual immorality? (Proverbs 6:26-35)

Give it some deeper thought . . .

Have you ever been tempted to commit adultery? What was it you hoped to gain through an adulterous affair? Was your expectation reasonable?

What things can you change about your thought life that will make it easier to avoid this kind of temptation?

Get together and talk about it . . .

1. All of us know someone who has committed adultery. From your observations, what have been some of the consequences of that behavior?

2. We live in a hyper-romanticized culture. Why do you think that is? How do television and movies contribute to unreasonable expectations for romance?

3. What do you think people are looking for when they commit adultery? Is it the same for men as it is for women?

4. What keeps you from committing adultery? Do you think it would ever be possible for you to fall into this sin?

Putting it into action . . .

Most men are not very romantic because no one has ever modeled or explained to them how to be. Some women refuse to tell their husbands what romance looks like to them because they feel it is "unromantic" to do so. So they remain frustrated.

Sit down together and discuss what romance "looks like" from your perspective. Then pray together, asking the Lord to help you implement actions into your relationship that would help you to more effectively communicate the love you have for one another.

Notes

Notes